sew baby

sew baby

cuddly and cute bibs, blankets, booties, and more

Choly Knight

Design Originals

an Imprint of Fox Chapel Publishing
www.d-originals.com

About the Author

Choly Knight is from Orlando, Florida. She has been crafting for as long as she can remember, and has drawn, painted, sculpted, and stitched everything in sight. She began sewing clothing in 1997 and has yet to put her sewing machine away. After studying studio art and earning a BA in English, she now enjoys trying to find numerous different ways to combine her passions for writing, fine art, and craft art. She created all of the designs, projects, and patterns appearing in this book. She focuses on handcrafted clothing, accessories, and other creations inspired by Japanese art, anime, and style, and specializes in cosplay (costume play) hats and hoodies. She sells her wares at anime conventions and in her Etsy shop: *www.Etsy.com/shop/ShoriAmeshiko.*

ISBN 978-1-57421-421-5

Library of Congress Cataloging-in-Publication Data

Knight, Choly.

  Sew baby / Choly Knight.

    pages cm

  Includes index.

  Summary: "Nothing is cuter than a baby, but this book comes close with simple and adorable sewing projects that are almost as cute as your little one! Step-by-step instructions, how-to photographs and approachable patterns show you how to add sweetness to the nursery with darling baby clothes, stuffed animal plushies and practical accessories. Eighteen easy-to-sew projects cover all of the basics that babies need for their first few years of growing. They feature charming applique faces inspired by the kawaii fashion sense-In Japanese, kawaii means cute, adorable, or loveable. Faces are one of the first things that babies are programmed to recognize, so why not surround them with lots of loving, handmade smiles? Projects range from very easy to intermediate, so they're simple to understand and come together quickly. All you need is a sewing machine, some inexpensive fabric, and a few basic sewing tools. So go ahead and create some beautiful toys and cute little clothes to make some lasting memories with your one-of-a-kind baby! "-- Provided by publisher.

  ISBN 978-1-57421-421-5 (pbk.)

  1. Infants' clothing. 2. Sewing. 3. Infants' supplies. I. Title.

TT637.K59 2013

646'.36--dc23

                    2012027556

© 2013 by Choly Knight and Design Originals, *www.d-originals.com*, an imprint of Fox Chapel Publishing, 800-457-9112, 1970 Broad Street, East Petersburg, PA 17520.

Printed in China
First printing

Introduction

For years I have been designing and sewing creations with a cute theme in mind, particularly the Japanese *kawaii* style (the style seen in Hello Kitty and other character creations). For so long I had geared my designs toward teens and college kids. Their eccentric and ironic sense of humor really went for my scary, nerdy, and funny *kawaii* style.

However, I was surprised to find that over the years, customers told me their babies and children were just as drawn to my cute accessories and plushies as adults were. Toddlers were swiping my quirky animal hats and parading around in them before their parents ever had a chance. I don't know why it never occurred to me to cater to youngsters alongside their adventurous parents, but before I knew it, I was receiving constant requests for baby merchandise.

I took the opportunity to create sweet baby projects for all the little ones in my life: nieces, nephews, and babies of friends and coworkers, and they all came back with rave reviews. Their babies were getting constant compliments about my animal hats, and toddlers refused to put down their new plush friends.

The designs in this book are inspired by many of the projects that were favorites among my customers and young mothers I know. As much as I love to design great items for parents, in this book I was able to indulge my softer side with more than a dozen sweet projects for little ones. I went less quirky and more cuddly, less snarky and more sweet, creating adorable yet sophisticated designs with loads of soft and snuggly members of the animal kingdom.

If there is one thing I've learned from young mothers, it is that they always know exactly what they want for their baby, but sometimes don't have time for it. I just know the projects here will help on both counts. Each project has several variations and can be easily customized to your tastes or personality. And each project is sure to come together quickly and easily during one or a few naptimes, meaning more time for playing and less time working.

I will never forget a story told to me by one of my uncles. He was a professional artist, and over the years had noticed that he frequently used a hexagon pattern in his graphic designs. He realized he must have had an affinity for it and adopted it as a kind of signature mark. One day, he helped my grandparents move by cleaning out the attic and he and my grandmother came across an old baby quilt. My grandmother explained that my great-grandmother had made the quilt for him, and for nights on end she rocked him gently to sleep while wrapped in that fabric. When my uncle unraveled the quilt, he discovered it was an intricately hand-pieced hexagon piece, made of dozens of the shape that had stuck in his creative mind so much.

It amazed me how something so simple and sweet can have such a life-changing affect on a person. And I wrote this book hoping that maybe you will one day have the same experience with your baby. Maybe it will be a plaid quilt pattern, the colors of the mobile you create, or even just the warm smile on the plush friend that you stitch yourself. No matter what, these handmade creations are sure to create countless wonderful memories for you and your baby.

—Choly Knight

contents

getting started

The projects in this book require some very basic sewing techniques, so if you are familiar with sewing you can look through this section to get refreshed on the basic skills you'll be using. If you're not so familiar with sewing, however, this chapter is great to get you acquainted with some indispensible information about skills, techniques, and fabrics.

Each project is given a level of difficulty that takes into account the time and complexity of the techniques used. If you want to get the most out of this book, start out with the very easy projects and work your way up. You'll find that each chapter starts with the easiest project and works up to the most complex.

LEVEL: Very Easy

Ideal for first projects. Very quick to put together and requires just a few techniques.

LEVEL: Easy

A few more skills than a very easy project, but just as simple to put together.

LEVEL: Experienced Beginner

Some techniques might require some concentration to get it right, but the construction is still straightforward.

LEVEL: Intermediate

For those who already know basic sewing techniques and how to use a pattern.

These projects represent the four difficulty levels found in this book. The Floating Friends Mobile (upper left) is Very Easy; the Fluffy Fat Plushie (upper right) is Easy; the Patchwork Plushie (lower left) is Experienced Beginner; and the Cozy Critters Baby Booties (lower right) are Intermediate.

Fabrics

While you'll want to look over the instructions for a project before jumping in, you are probably itching to buy some fabric or maybe already have some lying in wait to use. Babies are quite pampered when it comes to fabric selection; you'll find a plethora of options designed just for little bodies. However, don't be afraid to pick fabrics that are less juvenile. Sophisticated colors look just as adorable with sweet faces as do classic pastels and primaries.

Fabrics that might seem very dull will be easily livened up with all the appliqué demonstrated in this book. The only real rule is to keep it fun! Babies are developing their vision during these crucial years and they deserve a whole palette of colors to explore.

For the sake of practicality, try to pick fabrics that are soft and comfortable to wear. Also be sure to wash all your fabrics before sewing with them in case they shrink.

Fabrics in the United States tend to come in widths of 45" (1145mm) and 60" (1525mm). The project materials list will make note of this difference in the fabric requirements. Make sure to check your fabric width when buying so you get the right amount. When the project does not mention fabric width, then either width is suitable. Below are some of the fabrics you'll encounter while checking out the projects.

Cotton

A classic staple for quilts, accessories, and clothing alike, cotton is all-natural, so it's light and breathable for baby. It comes in a variety of colors and patterns, sews easily, and often gets softer with every wash.

Flannel

A close runner-up to cotton is flannel, which is much thicker and warmer, but also softer than cotton. You'll find nearly as many baby prints in flannel as cotton, and it is a nice alternative when searching for something a little heftier.

Canvas & Twill

More utilitarian than a lot of the other fabrics encountered in this book, canvas and twill are fabrics for sturdier projects. These are not used for any baby clothes or toys in this book, but the medium-weight woven fabrics are excellent for standing up to lots of use and abuse, which is always a plus with a baby around.

Corduroy

An often-overlooked fabric thought only for adult clothes, corduroy has a plush softness in its ridges that is a delight for baby to touch. The lighter-weight, thinner cords are very easy to work with and often come in bright and fun colors, too. It's also a sturdy fabric.

Felt

Set slightly apart from other fabrics, felt is typically thought of more for crafting and accessories. Its fibers are neither woven nor knit, but rather intensely compressed to form a sheet. Because of this, using high-quality woolen felt is always best, as the fibers will be less likely to separate over time. And because felt does not fray, it is perfect for tiny embellishments and details.

Terry cloth

Terry cloth is a fabric that really works double time. Many new varieties are extremely soft and colorful, and in addition they work to clean up little spills and messes along the way. Cut-up towels work beautifully as a substitute, and using a bit of terry cloth in just about any project is a wonderful way to be sure your baby is always clean and spotless.

Fleece

Fleece is an excellent all-around fabric, suitable in dozens of applications. It's soft, has just the right amount of stretch, and doesn't fray, so it works well for toys, accessories, and clothing. It's also easy to sew and washes well, so if other fabrics are tricky and not agreeing with you, you can always fall back on fleece to turn out a great product.

Interlock knit

While stretch knits can come in various materials and thicknesses, interlock knit is an excellent standard for working with baby projects. It's a slightly heftier weight while still having the comfortable T-shirt-like texture that everyone loves. Try to go with materials that have a high-cotton content for the best feel.

Minky

A real luxury for your baby, minky is a kind of faux fur similar in construction to fleece. The feel, however, is remarkably soft and delightful. It comes in lots of bright colors and piles, from short and smooth to shaggy and long to novelty designs like diamonds and stripes.

Basic Sewing Tools

You can get through just about any project in this book with the most basic sewing tools one would usually have in a sewing kit. Some other, more specialty tools are useful to have to make the process easier and quicker, so look through them here if you feel like you want to add them to your arsenal.

Sewing machine

A reliable sewing machine with a straight and zigzag stitch can do wonders and master all the projects in this book. Stitch length and width adjustment is also a plus, and built-in decorative stitches can be put to good use for a lot of embellishments here.

Sewing shears

Sharper and of higher quality than standard scissors, sewing shears are indispensible for cutting crisp pieces from your fabric.

Sewing pins

Pins are important for cutting patterns and setting up your fabric for seaming. All varieties work well, but keep in mind that some plastic types will melt under an iron.

Sewing machine needles

Machine needles can vary depending on the fabric you're using. A universal needle works well for most projects, but if you're encountering skipped stitches or broken thread, try a needle that better suits what you're sewing. You'll find needles are categorized by fabric weight and whether

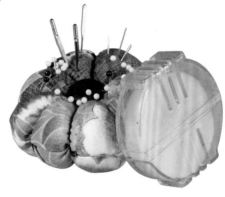

Needles and pins. Needles and pins are one of those items you'll probably need more than you think. Having a plethora of needles and pins for hand and machine makes sewing work much smoother, and beeswax can take a lot of headache out of hand sewing too.

the fabric is woven or knit. Remember to change needles often, usually after every project, to prevent them from becoming too dull and breaking.

Hand-sewing needle

Standard hand-sewing needles or "sharps" come in a variety of sizes. Find the size that best suits you and your fingers.

Threads

All-purpose thread works wonderfully for about every project here. Other options are embroidery thread, usually made from rayon, which offers a sleeker and shinier look for any embroidery work that you'd like to stand out.

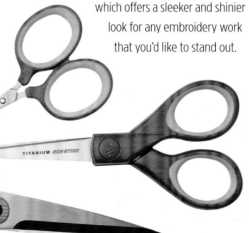

Sewing shears are essential for every sewing project. Large sewing shears are best for cutting large pieces of fabric down to the appropriate dimensions, but you can also purchase medium and small shears for trimming smaller pieces of fabric and thread. Always take good care of your sewing shears and they'll stay sharp through many projects.

Tape measure or ruler

Measuring is crucial when sewing to be sure that the projects will fit your baby perfectly or that the fabric piece you're cutting is precise.

Iron

An iron is better than just about any other tool to make a project look more professional. Pressing seams, corners, and curves with a steam iron makes all the difference in making your projects look better and come together easier.

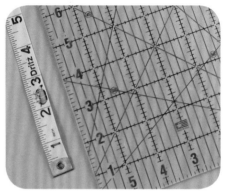

Tape measures and rulers. Get the most accurate cuts with a good tape measure or quilting ruler.

Seam ripper

A seam ripper is always a good tool to have around in case of mistakes.

Fabric marker

Sewing can be a lot like a puzzle, and fabric markers make it easier to put those puzzle pieces together. They make marks for seams or embellishments, and being water and air soluble makes them worth their weight in gold.

Carbon tracing paper & wheel

An alternative to fabric markers is carbon tracing paper and a tracing wheel. First, the carbon paper and fabric is stacked, and then the wheel is run along the pattern guidelines. This transfers carbon marks to the fabric, which can be washed away later.

Additional Supplies

In addition to basic tools and fabric, some projects call for special supplies. Some are called notions, others embellishments, but all are quite standard, easy to find, and helpful to keep around for other projects in the future.

Small and important tools. Smaller tools like fabric markers, tracing wheels, and seam rippers often go overlooked in a sewing basket, but are truly vital for making your project just to your taste.

Rotary cutter

Working much like a pizza cutter, a rotary cutter is a sharp-bladed tool that can cut long straight lines in a snap. It's a boon for quilting, and works best with a ruler to keep cuts straight and a mat underneath to protect surfaces from the sharp blade.

Pinking shears

Woven fabrics like cotton and flannel tend to unravel when their edges are left raw. A fast way of finishing those edges is with pinking shears, which cut the fabric in a zigzag pattern and prevent the edges from fraying to bits.

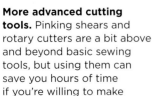

More advanced cutting tools. Pinking shears and rotary cutters are a bit above and beyond basic sewing tools, but using them can save you hours of time if you're willing to make the investment.

Ribbon

Ribbon is not only adorable for embellishment, but also for practical uses such as hanging a mobile. It comes in many widths and colors, so it can add a distinctive look to your project.

Hook-and-loop tape

Hook-and-loop tape is a simple kind of closure to use for baby, because it doesn't require any fiddling with buttons, zippers, or snaps. Go with the sew-on variety to make sure it stays put against prying fingers.

Elastic

Braided and knit elastic closures make it very easy to slip items on and off of your baby. You might come across plush elastic, which has a soft and fuzzy underside, or lingerie elastic, which has a decorative picot edge. Whether it's comfort or extra details, they both would work perfectly for the Sweet Bottoms Baby Bloomers (page 57) project.

Batting

Polyester batting is a definite go-to filling for toys and plush animals. While other fillings, such as micro pellets, are available for purchase, these choices can be dangerous for a baby because the pellets can be swallowed.

Quilt batting

This long and thin sheet of batting is made specifically for quilts. The polyester varieties are much fluffier, while the cotton varieties are thinner and denser. They typically come in packages for a specific blanket size or by the yard.

Beeswax

While not absolutely necessary for most projects, beeswax is useful for adding strength to thread for hand sewing. Running thread along a beeswax block coats it and prevents breaking and knots. But the real advantage of strengthening the thread is to prevent baby fingers from prying off embellishments and other hand-sewn parts of projects.

Fusible web

Used in this book for appliqué, fusible web is a paper-backed adhesive that is adhered to your selected fabric with an iron. After peeling the paper away, the adhesive is left behind and can then be ironed to another surface. I recommend the lightweight variety, as the heavyweight variety is for appliqué that isn't meant to be sewn—and I recommend that all embellishments and appliqués be sewn down sturdily to prevent them from coming loose and getting into any baby's mouths. Fusible web is sold by the yard and in packages. See how fusible web is used in the "Appliqué Techniques" feature (page 16).

Stabilizer

Stabilizer is often used in tandem with fusible web for the appliqué process. The dense stitches from appliqué can often warp or put strain on fabric. Stabilizer prevents that from happening. Light- to medium-weight stabilizer is best for these projects, because the leftover margins can be torn away after use.

Sewing Techniques and Terms

Phrases such as these might pop up in the directions for your project, and if you don't know what they mean, this is a good place to start to get the jargon cleared up.

Hand sewing

Just a bit of hand sewing practice can get you through the projects in this book. To the right are the stitches that come up most frequently.

Pattern symbols and guidelines

Pattern guidelines and symbols may differ, so it always helps to read over patterns and instructions before jumping into a project. The patterns from this book will list seam allowances, fold lines, seam lines, and grain lines. The circle symbols indicate where seams break and an opening is left, and gray lines show where to place appliqué or other project pieces. Mark these on your fabric using tracing paper or a fabric marker. The patterns will also indicate how many of each piece to cut, and in what color and fabric if it's helpful for the look of the project.

Seam allowance

This is the space between the edge of your fabric and where the seam is made. The standard for most U.S. patterns is ⅝" (16mm), though it can vary depending on the project and how small it is. Always check the pattern to know what your seam allowance is.

Grain line

The grain line of a fabric follows the direction in which the fabric was knitted or woven and goes parallel to the selvedge (the machine-finished edges of the fabric). The pattern pieces have a grain line arrow that indicates how the pattern piece should be placed to ensure proper stretching and drape in the right directions.

Basting stitch. This long, even stitch, also known as a running stitch, is used to temporarily hold fabric together. To sew this, weave your needle up and down through the fabric to make stitches about 1" (25mm) apart. Pull the thread lightly and do not let it gather up. This can also be done by machine with a very long straight stitch.

Ladder stitch. This is a bit of a crisscrossing stitch that sews two edges of fabric together neatly. It is used heavily for plushies. To sew this, stick your needle into the fold of one edge and bring it back out about ⅛" (3mm) down the fold. Go across to the other side and repeat, creating a ladder effect with the crossing threads. Pull tightly and the threads disappear into the fabric.

Whip stitch. This is a rapid overhand stitch meant to quickly bring two edges together while encasing the ends. To sew this, wrap the thread from the front of the fabric to the back and stick the needle toward you. Do this again about ⅛" (3mm) away from the last point. Continue and the thread will continually wrap around the fabric.

Finishing edges

The raw edges of woven fabrics tend to unravel and fray apart if left unfinished. If you are using woven fabrics in your project, any exposed edges should be finished. This can be done with pinking shears, a zigzag stitch within the seam allowance, or with fray-blocking liquid.

Clipping corners and curves

When sewing pieces that will be turned right-side out, the seam allowances of convex corners and curves should be clipped or trimmed to accommodate excess fabric when the shape is inverted. Alternately, the seam allowances of concave corners and curves should be clipped or trimmed to accommodate the fabric stretching when the shape is inverted.

Hems

Single- and double-fold hems are the type of hems used for the projects in this book. This type of hem is done by folding the fabric by the measurement indicated in the directions either once or twice and ironing to make a firm crease. Sew the fold down and the hem is complete. A double-fold hem finishes the raw edge.

Darts

The darts used for the projects in this book are triangle-shaped tucks made in the fabric to create a pronounced, three-dimensional shape in the fabric piece. These are made by folding the triangle mark in half and sewing along the one half of the triangle. If the dart is big enough, cut it open and press the halves outward. If not, press it to one side.

Finishing edges. Certain fabrics can sometimes unravel when worked with or washed. Prevent this with pinking shears, a zigzag stitch, or fray-blocking liquid.

Clipping corners and curves. Seam allowances of curves and corners should be clipped before turning the pieces right side out.

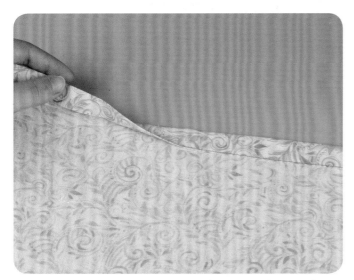

Hems. Single- and double-fold hems are used in this book for pockets and unfinished edges.

Darts. Used in the book for toys and the like, darts create a three-dimensional shape in otherwise two-dimensional fabric.

Appliqué Techniques

Appliqué is the main embellishment technique for the projects in this book, and there are many different ways to go about it. You can choose which method suits your skill level, resources, or the look you're going for.

Fabrics

Just about any fabric can be used as appliqué, but the ones used most frequently in this book are felt, fleece, flannel, and cotton. Be aware of whether your appliqué fabric unravels or not, as this will determine whether your appliquéd shapes will eventually have frayed edges. Use the satin stitch or zigzag stitch technique to cover raw edges and prevent fraying.

Supplies

Fusible web and stabilizer are two helpful supplies to use while appliquéing. Fusible web allows you to adhere your appliqué pieces to the main fabric to prevent shifting. It is indispensible for very tiny pieces. For much larger fabric pieces it might not be necessary, especially if you feel confident that the fabric can stay put while you sew.

Stabilizer keeps the main fabric from warping or stretching while you appliqué on it, and is especially important when using the satin stitch or sewing on stretchy fabrics like knits and fleece. Stabilizer is therefore less important (and can be skipped sometimes) when using the straight stitch or zigzag stitch, particularly on sturdy woven fabrics. Learn more about how to use these in the "Basic Sewing Tools" section (page 12).

Techniques

The satin stitch method completely encases the raw edge in thread, so nearly every fabric can be used. Also note that the stitches will cover the fabric entirely, so choosing complementary thread for a different look is an option. Embroidery threads also look very nice with this option, as the finished result has a bright sheen to it.

Straight stitch. After applying the appliqué pieces, sew a short straight stitch around the edge of the pieces. This will leave a raw edge, so choose your fabric accordingly. Lightweight stabilizer is recommended if you are appliquéing onto a knit fabric.

Zigzag stitch. After applying the appliqué pieces, sew a medium width and slightly short length zigzag stitch around the edge of the pieces. This will leave a slightly raw edge, which may fray or get fuzzy depending on how much your fabric unravels. Lightweight stabilizer is recommended if you are appliquéing onto a knit fabric.

Satin stitch. After applying the appliqué pieces, sew a medium to wide width and very short (usually the shortest your machine can handle) zigzag stitch around the edge of the pieces. This takes more patience and careful coordination, but yields a very professional result. Medium-weight stabilizer is recommended as the stitches can get very dense.

Sewing for Baby

When you know that your recipient will be a little one, there are a few extra thoughts to consider before starting with a project.

On sizes

A lot of the projects in this book are for decorative items and toys that your baby won't be wearing, but for the projects your baby will be putting on, the patterns will fit babies from around three months to nine months. Using knit fabrics, elastics, and other stretchy notions means the clothing and accessories can stretch out to fit babies in a decent range of shapes and ages. But if you would like to extend the life of one of the clothing patterns beyond nine months, enlarge the pattern by five to ten percent more to accommodate older babies and toddlers.

Fabric choice

It should come as no surprise that softer is always better when it comes to babies. At such a young age, babies rarely need clothes and toys that have to stand up to roughhousing or the like, so toughness can be compromised for comfort. Sometimes when it seems like a baby is crying for no reason, it could be that their clothes are uncomfortable, a decal or tag is scratching them, or something is cinched too tight. Better to avoid issues like that altogether and try and get the softest and coziest fabric available. Luckily it's not hard to find extraordinarily soft baby fabrics in every pattern and design you can imagine.

Stretchy fabrics are also a huge help with little growing bodies. Something a baby would otherwise grow out of in a few months can be held onto for a little while longer. Stain-resistant fabrics also make for easy care and washing.

On embellishments

It's tempting to take advantage of all the adorable embellishments stores provide for baby crafts, such as bows, buttons, patches, and other kinds of trinkets. Keep in mind, however, that babies love to explore the world with their mouths. Their tiny yet persistent fingers might find ways to pry those embellishments off if they aren't sewn as strongly as possible. For that reason, it is recommended that no embellishments be glued on or adhered with fusible web only. Every embellishment for these projects is either hand or machine sewn. For extra insurance when hand sewing, the thread can be doubled over or strengthened with beeswax.

Also avoid using drawstrings or any long lengths of ribbon or string in projects meant for babies. They can present a choking hazard and should be kept out of a baby's reach. Closures such as snaps, hook-and loop-tape, and buttons are better options.

for the nursery

When your baby finally comes home, it's hard to resist completely decking out his or her new room. It can become time-consuming and expensive to go all-out, but the projects from this chapter are great for making bold, bright statements that easily create a theme with little effort or cost. There are warm quilts, a mobile with lots of cute character options, and a toy organizer that's useful for kids of any age. The styles are eye-catching enough for a baby, but sweet and simple enough that they are sure to be favorites for years to come.

Floating Friends Mobiles, page 20.
Let the parliament of owls on this charming
mobile float your baby off to sleep. →

Floating Friends Mobiles

LEVEL: Very Easy

Pattern on page 102.

No baby's crib would be complete without an adorable mobile. Assembling all of the little bits is so easy—the only hard part is deciding which characters to pick and how to decorate them. The pattern includes pieces for stormy clouds, robots, and owls, and they can be varied with swappable features and embroidery to make each one different. But don't be afraid to use embellishments you have on hand, such as buttons, ribbon, rickrack, or other colorful found items. These little friends use very little fabric, so there's the option to make just a few or a whole army. And don't think they'll need to be stashed away when baby has gotten too old for a mobile. Cut them free from their hangings, stitch on a ribbon, and these little plush friends make great charms!

This project uses felt, making it easy to work very small without worrying about the fabric fraying. Synthetic felt works just fine for this, but any felt that is 100 percent wool or part wool is definitely better. Felt with wool content cuts cleaner and maintains its shape better over time.

Sew Much More!

Make a Chinese Zodiac mobile using the patterns from the Chinese Zodiac Headbands (see pages 110–111).

MATERIALS

- For clouds, raindrops, and lightning bolts: 9" x 12" (230 x 305mm) sheets of felt in blue, aqua, yellow, gray, and black
- For robots: 9" x 12" (230 x 305mm) sheets of felt in two contrasting colors (or more for variety)
- For owls: 9" x 12" (230 x 305mm) sheets of felt in two contrasting colors and white (or more for variety)
- Matching thread
- Batting
- Fusible web
- Stabilizer
- Clear filament
- 8" (205mm) embroidery hoop (inner hoop)
- 6 yds. (6m) of ⅝" (16mm) ribbon

TOOLS

- Fabric scissors
- Fabric pins
- Fabric marker
- Large hand-sewing needle
- Glue

Variation: Robots.

Variation: Storm Clouds.

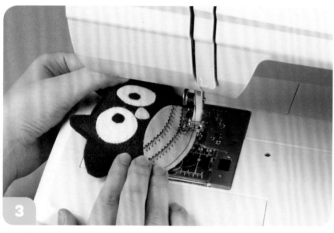

1

Appliqué the features. Cut the pattern pieces from the fabric and make any markings. Apply fusible web to the appliqué pieces and apply them to the fronts of the characters. [For owls: Hand- or machine-sew a V pattern on the stomach. Decorative machine stitches also work great for this.]

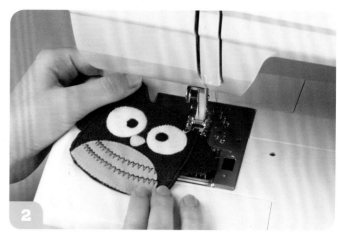

2

Sew the body pieces. With wrong sides together, sew the front character pieces to the back. Insert arms, legs, ears, or wings as indicated and leave an opening where the circle markings indicate for stuffing.

3

Stuff and close the characters. Stuff the characters lightly with batting. Sew closed the opening left on each character. [For robots: Slip the opening of the body into the opening of the head and sew the head closed through all the layers.] Repeat Steps 1–3 for as many characters as desired.

4

Thread the characters. Thread the filament through the sewing needle. Thread the filament through each body. Create a chain of characters as desired by knotting the filament at the top of one character and bottom of the next character and repeating the process.

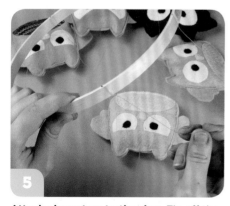

5

Attach characters to the ring. Tie off the filament from each character around the embroidery hoop. Secure tightly and add a dab of glue on the knot for insurance.

6

Wrap the ring with ribbon. Use the ⅝″ (16mm) ribbon to wrap the embroidery hoop, securing the beginning and end with glue. Be sure to go around each filament knot and cover the hoop completely.

7

Wrap more ribbon for hanging. Wrap more ribbon around four points on the hoop. Sew the ribbons together about 8″ (205mm) from the end to make a bow, or simply make an overhand knot. Suspend the mobile from the ceiling out of the baby's reach and watch your little one delight in the show!

Pirate Isle Toy Organizer

LEVEL: Experienced Beginner

Pattern on pages 103–104.

This versatile organizer more than earns its keep. The deep, wide pockets are great for holding all kinds of items. Hang it off the changing table and use it for holding wipes, washcloths, and other hygiene supplies, or use it to hold toys as your baby gets older and learns about cleaning up. The hanging loops can be used to hang the organizer from installed hooks, or off a bar. All that, and the adorable pirate characters won't lose their appeal for quite some time! They're perfect if your baby already has an older sibling to share with. With that said, make sure to pick good, sturdy fabric like linen or twill for the body of the organizer so it can stand up to all the great toys that will be stuffed into it! Piecing together all the appliqué characters can be the tricky part of this project, so follow the tips for "Appliquéing a Picture" (page 28) and it will be a breeze.

MATERIALS

Appliqué fabric:
- Fat quarter of red cotton
- Fat quarter of white cotton
- Fat quarter of black cotton
- Fat quarter of gray cotton
- Fat quarter of pink cotton
- Fat quarter of brown cotton
- Fat quarter of dark brown cotton
- Fat quarter of yellow cotton
- Fat quarter of green cotton
- Fat quarter of tan cotton
- Fat quarter of purple cotton

TOOLS
- Fabric scissors
- Fabric pins
- Fabric marker
- Large hand-sewing needle

- ½ yd. (½m) linen or twill for organizer pockets
- 1½ (1½m) yd. linen or twill for main organizer and straps
- Four ¾–1" (20–25mm) buttons
- Thread to match appliqué fabrics
- Thread to match main fabrics
- Fusible web
- Stabilizer

Cut the various rectangle and square pattern pieces from the fabric following the chart below:

Fabric Color	Size to Cut	Number to Cut	Seam Allowance
Vertical Pockets	10½" x 11½" (270 x 290mm)	3	1¼" (30mm)
Horizontal Pockets	15" x 10½" (380 x 270mm)	2	1¼" (30mm)
Backing	31¼" x 23¼" (795 x 590mm)	2	⅝" (15mm)
Straps	3¼" x 11¼" (85 x 290mm)	4	⅝" (15mm)

These illustrations will give you an idea of how to layer your appliqué pieces.

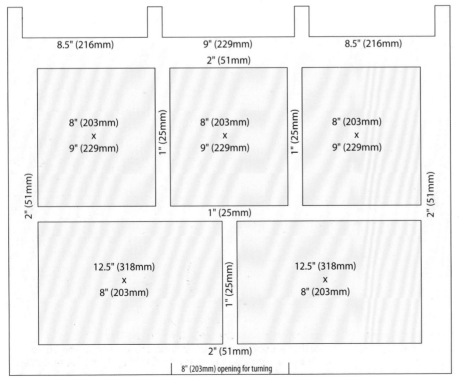

This illustration shows how the pockets and straps should be laid out for proper spacing.

Iron the edges of the pockets. Turn down the edges of each pocket by ⅝" (16mm) and iron them flat. Repeat this again to give each pocket finished edges.

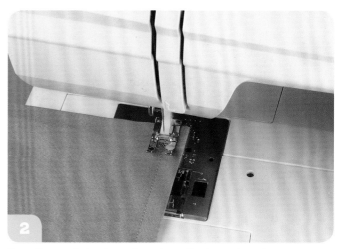

Hem the pocket edges. Sew along the top edge of every pocket fold to hem it in place.

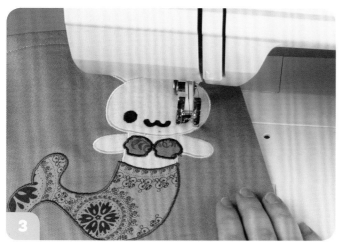

Appliqué the characters. Cut out the appliqué fabric pieces from the pattern and apply fusible web. Iron and sew the pieces in place using the character layout guide (page 26).

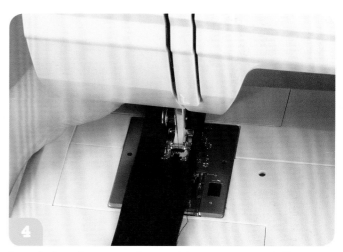

Sew the hanging straps. Sew each hanging strap in half lengthwise to make a long tube. Turn inside out and press flat.

Baste the straps. Fold each strap into a loop and baste along the top of the organizer, spacing them evenly as shown by the illustration (page 26).

Sew the organizer backing. Sew the two backing pieces together around the edges, leaving an opening at the bottom for turning right side out. Turn the backing right side out, press, and sew the opening closed.

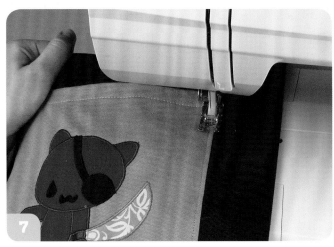

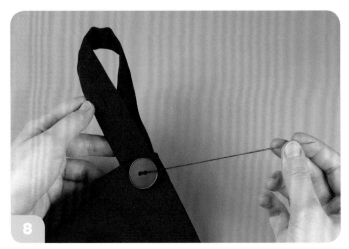

Attach the pockets. Space out and pin the pockets in place following the illustration. Sew each pocket in place along the sides and bottom, leaving the top open.

Attach the buttons. Strongly sew buttons in place behind each strap. To hang, wrap each strap over a rod or bar and loop over the button. Then stuff full of toys and other goodies!

Appliquéing a Picture

You can make a big impact with just a little bit of fabric through appliqué, especially when you use enough to construct a picture. Keeping track of and arranging all those little bits of fabric can be a headache, so here are some tips to make it easier. Your appliqué pieces will be adhered to the fusible web all at once, and you're free to cut them out when you're ready to use them so they won't get lost in the meantime.

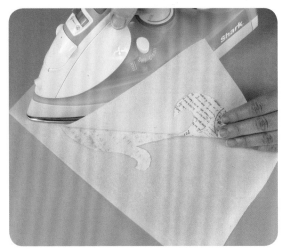

Iron your appliqué fabrics to the fusible web all at once. Get a sheet of parchment paper and lay out your appliqué pieces wrong side up. Take your fusible web and spread it carefully over the appliqué pieces, being sure not to shift them into each other. Then, iron down the entire sheet. When the paper cools, you'll be able to peel it easily from the appliqué pieces.

Apply the fusible web first, then trace the shapes. Iron your fusible web to your appliqué fabric before cutting out the pieces. Trace the pattern pieces, again wrong side up, onto the paper with a pencil. You will then be able to cut them out, paper and all, with more stability than if they were just fabric. This is great for extremely tiny pieces!

Plaid Quilt

LEVEL: Intermediate

Pattern on page 105.

A baby's nursery or sleeping space would be incomplete without lots of cozy quilts. This quilt works beautifully for snuggling or as a wall hanging. The easy-to-build plaid pattern can take on so many looks just by varying the color scheme. Go with violet for a sweet girly look or classic red for a sophisticated look. Hunter green becomes as warm and boyish as grandpa's old flannel shirt, and hot pink is perfect for one wild and crazy baby. Add the optional monogram for an extra personal touch—a real plus if giving the quilt as a gift. The finished quilt size is 36" x 48" (915 x 1220mm).

The plaid effect is created by choosing colors that are blends of their neighbors to simulate the woven stripes that go through a piece of plaid fabric. Adopting a monochromatic color scheme makes creating the palette much simpler. Here is a palette example that will make selecting your fabrics much more streamlined.

Fabric Name	Color
A	Light Green
B	Medium Green
C	Dark Green
D	Dark Pale Green
E	White
F	Gray
G	Black

MATERIALS

- ½ yd. (½m) cotton in Color A
- ¾ yd. (¾m) cotton in Color B
- ½ yd. (½m) cotton in Color C
- ½ yd. (½m) cotton in Color D
- Fat quarter cotton in Color E
- Fat quarter cotton in Color F
- Fat quarter cotton in Color G
- 1½ yds. (1½m) cotton for binding
- 1½ yds. (1½m) cotton for backing
- 38" x 50" (965 x 1270mm) quilt batting
- Thread to match quilt fabrics
- Fat quarter of appliqué fabric (optional)
- Thread to match appliqué fabric (optional)
- Fusible web (optional)
- Stabilizer (optional)

TOOLS

- Safety pins
- Fabric scissors
- Fabric pins
- Rotary cutter
- Quilting ruler

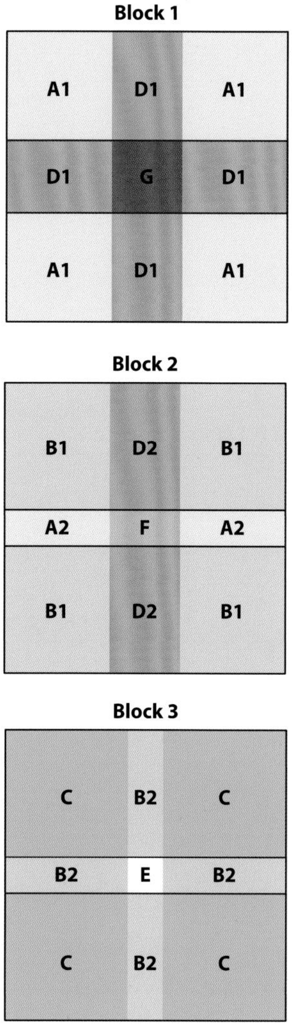

Block 1

A1	D1	A1
D1	G	D1
A1	D1	A1

Block 2

B1	D2	B1
A2	F	A2
B1	D2	B1

Block 3

C	B2	C
B2	E	B2
C	B2	C

Use this illustration to guide you in assembling your blocks.

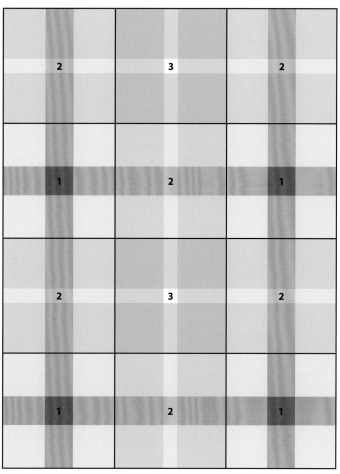

Use this illustration as a guide to correctly assemble the quilt blocks into rows and the finished quilt top.

Cut the various rectangle and square pattern pieces from the fabric following the chart below:

Fabric Color	Square Name	Size to Cut	Number to Cut	Seam Allowance
A	A1	5" x 5" (130 x 130mm)	16	¼" (6mm)
A	A2	5" x 2" (130 x 50mm)	12	¼" (6mm)
B	B1	5" x 5¾" (130 x 145mm)	24	¼" (6mm)
B	B2	2" x 5¾" (50 x 145mm)	8	¼" (6mm)
C	C	5¾" x 5¾" (145 x 145mm)	8	¼" (6mm)
D	D1	5" x 3½" (130 x 90mm)	16	¼" (6mm)
D	D2	3½" x 5¾" (90 x 145mm)	12	¼" (6mm)
E	E	2" x 2" (50 x 50mm)	2	¼" (6mm)
F	F	3½" x 2" (90 x 50mm)	6	¼" (6mm)
G	G	3½" x 3½" (90 x 90mm)	4	¼" (6mm)
Binding	Vertical	3½" x 54" (90 x 1370mm)	2	½" (15mm)
Binding	Horizontal	3½" x 44" (90 x 1120mm)	2	½" (15mm)

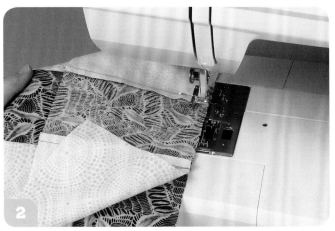

Make the strips for Block 1. Use the illustration as a guide to assemble Block 1. Sew a D1 square in between two A1 squares twice to create the top and bottom rows. Sew a G square in between two D1 squares to create the middle row.

Finish Block 1. Sew the middle row between the top and bottom rows to finish Block 1. Repeat Steps 1–2 three more times to create four of Block 1.

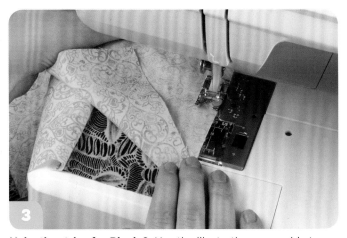

Make the strips for Block 2. Use the illustration as a guide to assemble Block 2. Sew a D2 square in between two B1 squares twice to create the top and bottom rows. Sew an F square in between two A2 squares to create the middle row.

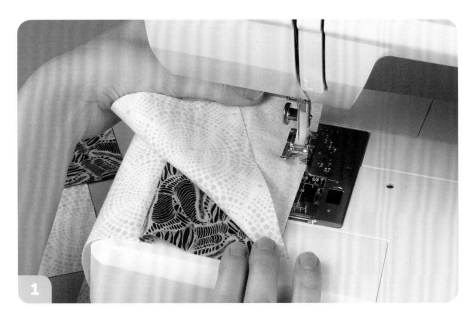

Finish Block 2. Sew the middle row in between the top and bottom rows to finish Block 2. Repeat Steps 3–4 five more times to create six of Block 2.

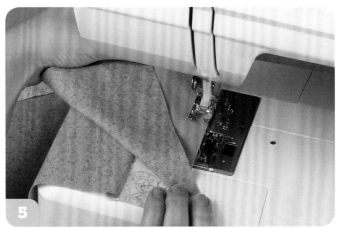

Make the strips for Block 3. Use the illustration as a guide to assemble Block 3. Sew a B2 square in between two C squares twice to create the top and bottom rows. Sew an E square in between two B2 squares to create the middle row.

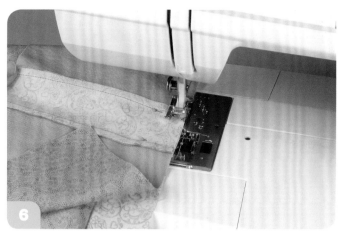

Finish Block 3. Sew the middle row in between the top and bottom rows to finish Block 3. Repeat Steps 5–6 once more to create two of Block 3.

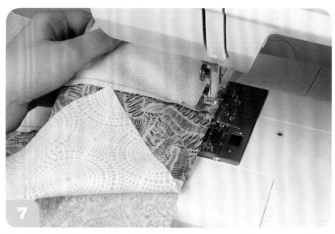

Sew the quilt rows. Use the illustration as a guide to assemble the rows for the quilt top. Sew Block 3 between two of Block 2. Sew Block 2 (rotated 90°) between two of Block 1. Repeat this once more to create 4 rows.

Assemble the quilt top. Use the illustration as a guide to assemble the quilt top from the rows. Sew each row to the next along the long sides, alternating them to create the quilt top.

Appliqué the monogram. Cut and apply fusible web to the appliqué fabric. Iron and sew the selected monogram letter to the bottom right corner of the quilt top, about 4" (100mm) in from the edge.

Baste the quilt layers. Stack the backing fabric, quilt batting, and quilt top (in that order) on a large flat surface. Smooth out as many wrinkles as possible and, working outward from the middle, begin pinning the layers together with safety pins every 5"–10" (130–255mm).

Quilt the layers. With a slightly longer straight stitch, sew through all the layers of the quilt along the edges of the blocks. Work from the center outward and smooth the fabric constantly, making sure all the layers are perfectly even. When it's complete, trim the excess quilt batting and backing sticking out from the quilt top.

Bind the edges. Using the guide for "Binding a Quilt" (page 34), bind the edges of the quilt to finish.

Binding a Quilt

For quilt projects, binding is typically the final step and doing it well pays high dividends. With a little bit of practice, it becomes much easier, and the process more intuitive. The squared-edge method is easier for beginners, while the mitered method produces a more professional look, but is a little more complex.

Squared-edge binding. The square-edged binding style looks professional, but is simple to accomplish.

Squared-Edge Binding:

1

Iron the binding. Fold all the binding pieces in half lengthwise, wrong sides together. This will result in narrower strips of binding.

2

Sew the side binding. Pin up the side binding to the front sides of the quilt, matching raw edges. The binding should run off the end of the edges of the quilt by several inches on each side. Sew the binding to the quilt sides using a ½″ (13mm) seam allowance. Trim the excess binding flush with the edge of the quilt.

3

Flip the side binding. Flip the side binding over toward the back side of the quilt. Fold the binding so it wraps around the edge and iron in place.

4

Finish the side binding. From the front of the quilt, sew along the edge of the binding seam line. This should catch the other edge of the binding from the back, finishing the binding for the sides.

5

Sew the top and bottom binding. Pin up the top and bottom binding to the top and bottom of the quilt matching raw edges. The binding should run off the end of the edges of the quilt by several inches on each side. Sew the binding to the quilt sides using a ½″ (13mm) seam allowance. Iron the binding away from the quilt.

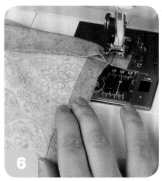

6

Sew the corners. Flip the binding back on itself and sew the edges about ⅛″ (3mm) away from the corner of the quilt. Trim the excess fabric.

7

Flip the top and bottom binding. Turn the corners inside out and flip the binding around the edge of the quilt. The newly sewn corners should now snugly encompass the corners of the quilt. Fold the rest of the binding so it wraps around the edge similar to Step 3. Iron in place.

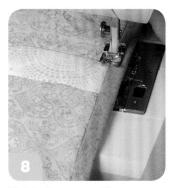

8

Finish the top and bottom. From the front of the quilt, sew along the edge of the binding seam line similar to Step 4. This should catch the other edge of the binding from the back, finishing the binding for the quilt.

Mitered-edge binding. The miter-edged binding style is more complex than the square-edged version, but is worth the extra effort.

Mitered-Edge Binding:

Chain all the binding pieces. Sew the four binding pieces together into a long line. Do this by sewing the the short ends together along the bias (45˚ to the grain)—it creates a less noticable join between the strips. Trim the excess fabric, unfold the fabric along the seam, and press it flat, which creates one long strip.

Iron the binding strip. Iron the entire binding strip in half, wrong sides together, to create one very long binding strip. This should be long enough to go around the edge of your quilt with about 12″ (305mm) or more leftover.

Begin the mitered corner. Starting from the middle bottom edge of the quilt, line up the binding about 6″ (150mm) in from the strip to the edge of the quilt with raw edges together. Using a ½″ (13mm) seam allowance, sew the binding to the quilt edge, stopping ½″ (13mm) from the corner and sewing out at a 45˚ angle toward the corner point.

Fold the mitered corner. Fold the strip at a 45˚ angle away from the quilt then back down, creating another fold that is flush with the quilt edge. Hold these folds in place in preparation for the next step.

Finish the mitered corner. Starting at the very edge of the quilt with very strong backstitches, sew the other half of the corner binding to the next edge of the quilt, still keeping the ½″ (13mm) seam allowance. Repeat Steps 3–5 for the other corners of the quilt, and stop about 6″ (150mm) short of reaching the beginning point.

Attach the ends. Find where the binding ends meet together while remaining flush with the quilt. Open the binding up and sew the ends together with right sides facing. Fold the binding back and sew it to the quilt the same as the rest of the binding.

Flip the binding. Open the binding out and away from the quilt front and iron open. Wrap the binding around the edge of the quilt and iron in place. The corners in back are folded much like an envelope to achieve the mitered look.

Finish the binding. From the front of the quilt, sew along the seam of the binding around the perimeter of the quilt. This should catch the edge of the binding from the other side, finishing the binding.

Argyle Quilt

LEVEL: Intermediate

Pattern on page 105.

This snuggly quilt is another excellent project for reflecting the personality of your baby. Argyle is a classic pattern that takes on many different looks depending on the color scheme. Pretty pastels are perfect for a sweet girl's quilt; warm, autumn colors make it cozy and inviting. Cool neutrals are sleek and sophisticated, and bold neon colors paired with black are funky and fun. This design also works wonderfully with the monogram from the Plaid Quilt project; it's completely optional but will definitely add a special touch. Either way, the look is anything but babyish, so both you and your baby will want to hold onto this blanket forever. The finished quilt size is 36¾" x 55" (935 x 1400mm).

MATERIALS

- 1¾ yds. (1¾m) cotton in Color A
- 1¼ yds. (1¼m) cotton in Color B
- 1¾ yds. (1¾m) cotton for binding
- 1¾ yds. (1¾m) cotton for backing
- 12 yds. (12m) ⅝" (16mm) ribbon
- 37" x 56" (965mm x 1422mm) quilt batting
- Thread to match quilt fabric
- Fat quarter of appliqué fabric (optional)
- Thread to match appliqué fabric (optional)
- Fusible web (optional)
- Stabilizer (optional)

TOOLS

- Fabric scissors
- Fabric pins
- Safety pins
- Rotary cutter
- Quilting ruler

To make the most of your quilt's color palette, be sure to choose fabrics and ribbon in light, medium, and dark shades. The color choices and order you put them in can be up to you, but the contrast in darkness will really make your fabric and ribbon pop!

Cut the various rectangle and square pattern pieces from the fabric following the chart below:

Fabric Color	Size to Cut	Number to Cut	Seam Allowance
A	13½" x 13½" (345 x 345mm)	12	¼" (6mm)
B	13½" x 13½" (345 x 345mm)	6	¼" (6mm)
Horizontal Binding	3½ " x 44" (90 x 1120mm)	2	½" (13mm)
Vertical Binding	3½" x 60" (90 x 1525mm)	2	½" (13mm)

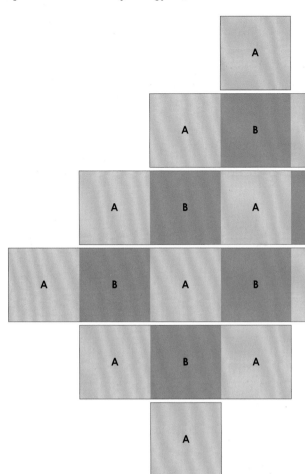

Use this illustration to correctly assemble your quilt squares into the diamond pattern.

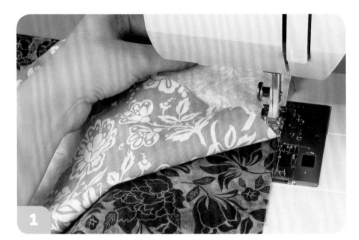

Sew block rows. Using the illustration as a guide, sew the rows of A and B squares. Sew one B square between two A squares twice (making two rows of three). Do the following twice: sew one A square between two B squares, then sew one more A square to each end (making two rows of five).

Finish quilt top. Using the illustration as a guide, sew the rows together. Sew the five-square rows together, sew the three-square rows to the outsides, then sew the last two squares to the corners.

Trim the quilt top. Turn the quilt top 45° so that each square now appears as a diamond. Trim the pointed edges of the squares so that the quilt top is now an even rectangle.

Baste the quilt layers. Stack the backing fabric, quilt batting, and quilt top (in that order) on a large flat surface. Smooth out as many wrinkles as possible and, working outward from the middle, begin pinning the layers together with safety pins every 5"–10" (130–255mm).

Quilt the layers. With a slightly longer straight stitch, sew through all the layers of the quilt along the edges of the squares. Work from the center outward and smooth the fabric constantly, making sure all the layers are perfectly even. When it's complete, trim the excess quilt batting and backing sticking out from the quilt top.

Bind the edges. Using the guide for "Binding a Quilt" (page 34), bind the edges of the quilt to finish.

Apply the ribbon. Pin the lengths of ribbon running down the middle of each square, going parallel to the squares' sides. Sew the ribbon down along the edges to complete the crisscrossing pattern.

Appliqué the monogram. Apply fusible web to the appliqué fabric. Appliqué the selected monogram letter to the bottom right corner of the quilt top, about 4" (100mm) in from the edge.

clothing

It seems like no matter what babies wear, they end up looking even more adorable than they already are. So why not have fun with lots of different exciting accessories like animal booties, hats, headbands, and bloomers? No matter what the look, baby can pull it off. All these projects feature cute animal motifs that make your baby look even cuddlier. People won't be able to help but lavish attention on such sweet styles. Each project uses very little fabric, making it easy to pamper your baby with fashions for every day of the week!

With animal hats, ducky booties, and zodiac
headbands, your baby will be covered in
snuggly handmade accessories. →

Fuzzy Menagerie Character Hats

LEVEL: **Easy**

Pattern on pages 106–109.

Everyone knows how important it is to keep a baby's head warm, so why not do it in a fun and adorable way? Trade in boring beanies for animal ears that are sure to put a smile on anyone's face. This project includes three great hat styles with ears and appliqués to make your baby look sweet as a button. The beanie-style hat offers a puppy, dragon, and panda; the earflap-style hat offers a bunny, raccoon, and owl; and the sleeping cap-style hat offers a seal, bird, and platypus. It might seem hard to pick which one to make, but luckily, you won't have to! With less than a yard of fabric for each hat, you can cover your baby's noggin with something new on a whim. Fleece works best for this project because it stretches just enough to fit cozily on growing babies.

Sew much more!

Swap out the face and ear patterns from the Bibs (pages 132–133), Hooded Towel (page 129), or Bloomers (page 113) projects for even more characters!

MATERIALS

For beanie hat (Panda, Dragon, and Puppy):
- ¼ yd. (¼m) of 60" (1525mm)-wide or ⅓ yd. (⅓m) of 45" (1145mm)-wide fleece
- ⅛ yd. (⅛m) or 12" x 12" (305 x 305mm) remnant of contrast color fleece

For earflap hat (Bunny, Owl, and Raccoon):
- ¼ yd. (¼m) of 60" (1525mm)-wide or ½ yd. (½m) of 45" (1145mm)-wide fleece
- *Additional for Raccoon:* ⅛ yd. (⅛m) or 12" x 12" (305 x 305mm) remnants of black and white fleece

For sleeping cap (Platypus, Bird, and Seal):
- ½ yd. (½m) fleece
- *Additional for Bird:* ⅛ yd. (⅛m) or 12" x 12" (305 x 305mm) remnant of yellow fleece
- *Additional for Platypus:* ¼ yd. (¼m) or 12" x 12" (305 x 305mm) remnant of contrast fleece

- Thread to match fleece fabrics
- Small amount of batting (for Bird and Dragon)
- Appliqué fabrics
- Thread to match appliqué fabrics
- Fusible web
- Stabilizer

TOOLS
- Fabric marker
- Hand-sewing needle
- Fabric scissors
- Fabric pins

↑ This adorable collection of beanie-style hats includes a dragon, puppy, and panda.

← ↓ These cuddly bird, seal, and platypus hats are shaped like a cozy sleeping cap.

← Precious bunny and raccoon caps sport warm earflaps for keeping your baby's head and ears out of the cold.

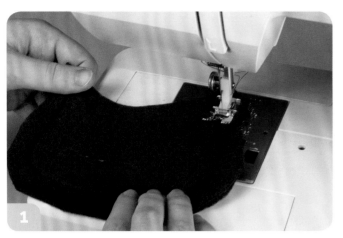

Sew all appendages. Sew the various appendages depending on the character: ears, fins, horns, wings, beak, or bill. Leave the bottom edges open for turning inside out or where an opening is indicated with circles on the pattern. Turn them right side out and press. [For Dragon: Hand-sew opening in wings closed.]

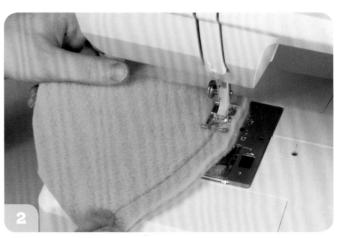

For beanie or earflap hat: Sew the crown quarters. Sew crown pieces in pairs, making two half circles.

For beanie or earflap hat: Sew the crown halves. Using the markings indicated by the pattern, insert the ear pieces in between the two crown halves. Sew the halves together, making the full hat crown. Iron the seam open.

For sleeping cap: Sew the cap top. Fold the sleeping cap top in half, and sew along the long curved edge. Leave the bottom straight edge open.

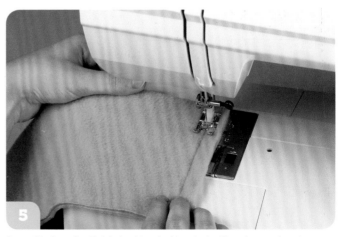

Sew the bands. Fold the band piece in half and sew the short ends together, creating a ring. Iron the seam open. [For beanie band: Fold in half, wrong sides together, lengthwise, and press flat.]

For earflap hat or sleeping cap: Sew the earflap bands together. Sew the two earflap band pieces together along the bottom curved edge. [For Platypus: Insert the platypus bill in between the earflap band pieces where indicated by the pattern.] Leave the flat edge along the top open. Clip corners and curves, turn right side out, and press.

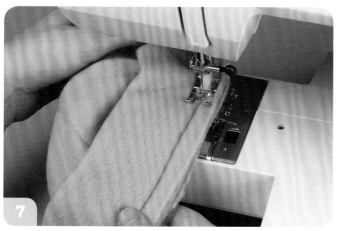

Sew the band to the crown. Pin the band around the crown piece, making sure back seams are matched up, and sew in place.

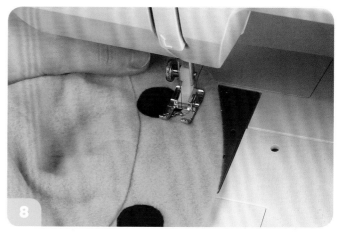

Appliqué the features. Cut and apply fusible web to the appliqué fabric. Iron and sew the appliqué pieces to the front of the hat. Follow the pattern guidelines for placement help.

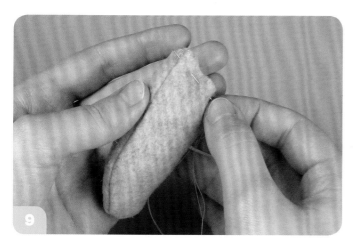

For Bird and Dragon: Prepare the stuffed features. Stuff the horns/beak with batting. Hand-sew a running stitch along the edge of pieces and cinch slightly closed.

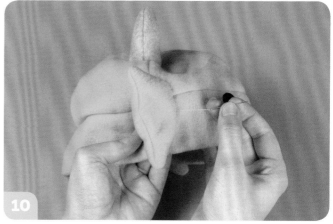

Hand-sew the extra features. Hand-sew the horns or beak to the faces of the dragon or bird. Also, hand-sew the dragon fins to the side and wings to the back. Attach any remaining additional pieces.

Chinese Zodiac Headbands

LEVEL: Easy

Pattern on pages 110–111.

While any baby is cute enough on his or her own, this adorable headband will be icing on the cake. It's adorned with little plush versions of each of the 12 Chinese zodiac animals—including the rat, ox, tiger, rabbit, dragon, snake, horse, goat, monkey, rooster, dog, and pig. The animals may be a little eccentric, but they're a great change from the typical flowers and bows that adorn most headbands. The band is also elasticized for snugness and softness. Whether you're a fan of Chinese culture, astrology, or just know a great conversation starter when you see one, these little characters are great for showing off the illustrious year when your baby was born. The face of each animal is made from fleece, while the details are made from felt. The headband itself is made from flannel for extra comfort, but cotton would work well, too.

Sew much more!

Skip the headband altogether and these little plush animals make great charms!

MATERIALS

Dog:
- 6" x 12" (150 x 305mm) square of tan fleece
- 9" x 12" (230 x 305mm) sheets of felt in black, white, and brown

Dragon:
- 6" x 12" (150 x 305mm) square of green fleece
- 9" x 12" (230 x 305mm) sheets of felt in black, green, and gray

Goat:
- 6" x 12" (150 x 305mm) square of gray fleece
- 9" x 12" (230 x 305mm) sheets of felt in black, gray, and cream

Horse:
- 6" x 12" (150 x 305mm) square of brown fleece
- 9" x 12" (230 x 305mm) sheets of felt in black and brown

Monkey:
- 6" x 12" (150 x 305mm) square of brown fleece
- 9" x 12" (230 x 305mm) sheets of felt in black and tan

Ox:
- 6" x 12" (150 x 305mm) square of brown fleece
- 9" x 12" (230 x 305mm) sheets of felt in black, tan, brown, and cream

Pig:
- 6" x 12" (150 x 305mm) square of pink fleece
- 9" x 12" (230 x 305mm) sheets of felt in black and pink

Rabbit:
- 6" x 12" (150 x 305mm) square of lavender fleece
- 9" x 12" (230 x 305mm) sheets of felt in black and lavender

Rat:
- 6" x 12" (150 x 305mm) square of gray fleece
- 9" x 12" (230 x 305mm) sheets of felt in black and gray

Rooster:
- 6" x 12" (150 x 305mm) square of white fleece
- 9" x 12" (230 x 305mm) sheets of felt in black, red, yellow, and white

Snake:
- 6" x 12" (150 x 305mm) square of green fleece
- 9" x 12" (230 x 305mm) sheets of felt in black and red

Tiger:
- 6" x 12" (150 x 305mm) square of orange fleece
- 9" x 12" (230 x 305mm) sheets of felt in black and white

- ⅛ yd. (⅛m) flannel fabric
- ½ yd. (½m) of ¾" (19mm) elastic
- Thread to match fleece, felt, and flannel fabrics
- Batting
- Fusible web

TOOLS

- Fabric scissors
- Fabric pins
- Fabric marker
- Hand-sewing needle
- Safety pins

An astrological gathering of astronomical size! This project
features designs for all twelve of the Chinese Zodiac animals.

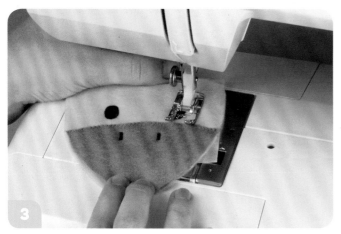

Appliqué the features. Cut and apply fusible web to the appliqué fabrics. Iron and sew the pieces to the bootie top where indicated by the pattern guidelines.

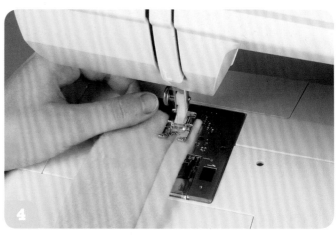

Sew the elastic casing. With wrong sides together, fold the back piece in half lengthwise and sew ½″ (13mm) from the fold to create an elastic casing.

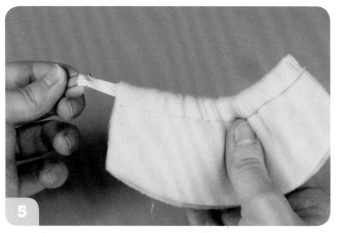

Insert the elastic. Cut the elastic to a 4″ (102mm) piece. Using a safety pin, thread the elastic through the casing, making sure to anchor each end of the elastic with basting stitches to each end of the casing.

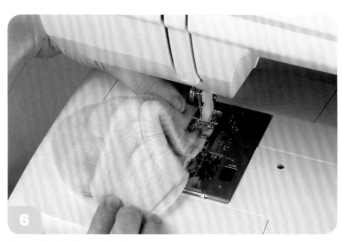

Baste the back to the front. [For Bunny: Baste bunny ears to the front piece, using guidelines indicated by the pattern.] Baste the short ends of the back to the top, matching up the side edges so they are flush.

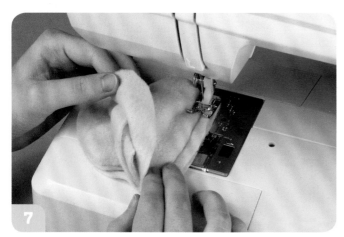

Sew the front pieces. Layer the second front piece over the first with right sides together. Sew along the same straight edge that was previously basted. Turn right side out for the full top piece of the bootie.

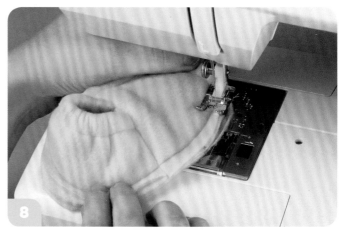

Sew the top to the sole. Match up the sole to the top of the bootie along the center back and front with right sides together. Sew along the edge, and keep in mind that the sole will have to be stretched at times to make the pieces match up. Repeat Steps 1–8 for the second bootie.

Sweet Bottoms
Baby Bloomers

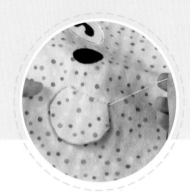

Pattern on page 113.

Diapers can be so plain and boring. Why not dress them up with these cute diaper covers? They're great for pulling together an outfit while still giving baby plenty of mobility, and the cute animal faces will have everyone impressed. The pattern includes pieces to make a puppy, fox, and bear (for little "bear" bottoms!). The tricky part of this project comes from applying the elastic to the waist and leg openings, but you'll find it goes easier if you accurately pin the pieces in place and sew a few inches at a time. Lots of fabrics are great for this project—jersey works well for extra stretch, cotton is breathable and has lovely patterns, and fleece is cuddly, warm, and probably the easiest with which to work.

Sew much more!

Swap out the face and ear patterns from the Bibs (pages 132–133), Character Hats (pages 106–109), or Hooded Towel (page 129) projects for even more characters!

MATERIALS

- ½ yd. (½m) of fleece, cotton, or jersey
- **For Fox:** 6" x 6" (150 x 150mm) scrap of black or contrast fabric
- **For Puppy:** 12" x 12" (305 x 305mm) scrap of brown contrast fabric
- Thread to match main fabrics
- 1½ yds. (1½m) of ⅜" (10mm)-wide elastic (picot-edged if available)
- Appliqué fabrics
- Thread to match appliqué fabrics
- Fusible web
- Stabilizer

TOOLS

- Fabric scissors
- Fabric pins
- Fabric marker
- Hand-sewing needle

Appliqué the animal face. Cut out and apply fusible web to the appliqué fabrics. Iron and sew them to the bloomer bottom following the pattern guidelines.

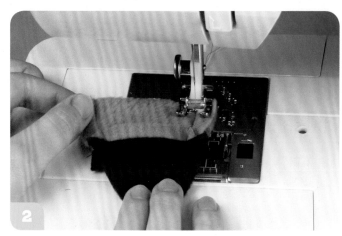

Sew the animal ears. [For Fox: Sew the ear base to the ear tips.] Sew the animal ear pieces together along the curved edge. Leave the straight edge open for turning right side out. Turn them right side out and iron lightly.

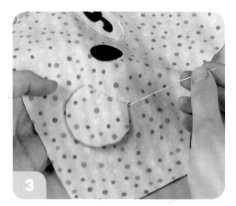

Sew the ears to the back. Turn the open edge of the ears under by about ⅜" (10mm). Hand-sew the bottom edge of the ear along the placement line indicated by the pattern. [For Puppy: Fold down the ears like a dog's and hand-sew the fold in place from the back.]

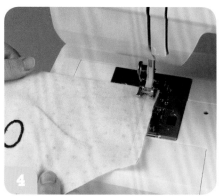

Sew the side seams. Fold the bloomers in half, right sides together. Match the short side edges and sew them together.

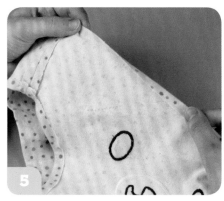

Fold under the waist and leg openings. Fold under the waist and leg openings by ⅜" (10mm) and iron firmly so the crease stays.

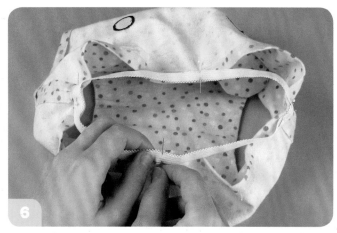

Pin the elastic. Cut the elastic into one 18" (460mm) and two 10" (255mm) pieces. Sew the ends together to make a loop. Pin the larger piece along the inside of the waist opening and the smaller pieces along the inside of the leg openings, matching up the half and quarter points because they will not be the same length. Make sure the picot edge peeks over the outside (if using).

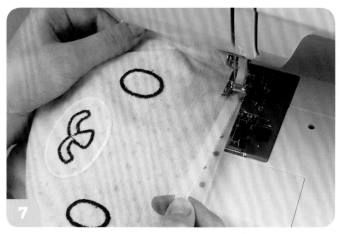

Apply the elastic. Using a wide and long zigzag stitch, sew the elastic to the openings. Stretch the elastic to make it fit along the openings. This will create a gathered effect.

3

toys

Every baby deserves lots of fun toys to delight and stimulate him or her. In here you'll find great plush animals, puppets, and other toys that are fantastic for hours of playtime and for training your baby's motor skills. Be prepared to find brand new friends that your baby won't want to let go of! Projects like the Fluffy Fat Plushie and the Lazy Body Pillow are bold, adorable, and work wonderfully as photo props. And projects like the Patchwork Plushies and Forest Friends Hand Puppets will easily become cherished keepsakes over the years. Overall, you'll find great and personal alternatives to expensive manufactured baby toys. You'll know they're safe for your baby because they don't contain choking hazards or plastic bits that can scratch, but most importantly, you'll know these soft friends come from the heart!

Make your baby's first best friend—
a fluffy stuffed animal, puppet,
or other cherished toy. ➔

Forest Friends Hand Puppets

LEVEL: Very Easy

Pattern on pages 114–115.

These sweet little hand puppets are incredibly easy to make. They're perfect for quickly entertaining your baby and to keep around when your child is old enough to create puppet shows. They can be whipped up so fast that it's easy to make the entire set. Make them in bright, patterned fabrics for a stylish look or soft, plush fabrics so they're fun to touch. Better yet, make them in terry cloth and they become the best bath buddies a baby could ask for. The pattern includes designs to make a raccoon, fox, and tiger, as well as some more aquatically inclined friends for washcloths: a duck, penguin, and frog.

Sew much more!

Swap out the face and ear patterns from the Patchwork Plushies (page 120) project for even more characters!

MATERIALS
- ⅓ yd. (⅓m) main fabric

For Frog:
- 6" x 6" (150 x 150mm) remnant of white fabric

For Penguin:
- ⅓ yd. (⅓m) or 6" x 12" (150 x 305mm) remnant of white fabric

For Fox, Tiger & Raccoon:
- ⅓ yd. (⅓m) or 12" x 12" (305 x 305mm) remnant of white fabric
- ⅓ yd. (⅓m) or 12" x 12" (305 x 305mm) remnant of black fabric

- Thread to match main fabrics
- Appliqué fabrics
- Thread to match appliqué fabrics
- Fusible web
- Stabilizer

TOOLS
- Fabric scissors
- Fabric pins
- Fabric marker

For Penguin, Fox, Raccoon, or Tiger: Sew the animal markings.
Sew the stomach marking to the front body piece using any desired appliqué technique. Center the stomach in the middle of the body and line up the bottom edges. [For Tiger: Sew the tiger stripes to the back using the pattern guidelines.]

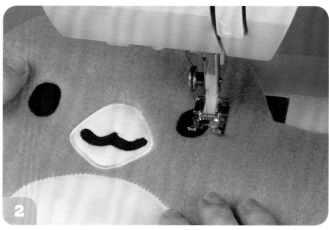

Appliqué the face. Cut and apply fusible web to the appliqué fabric. Iron and sew the appliqué pieces to the puppet body about 3" (75mm) from the top of the body piece. [For Frog: Appliqué the smile higher, about 1½" (40mm). Also appliqué the frog pupils to the frog eye pieces.]

For Fox, Raccoon, Tiger, or Frog: Sew the ears or eyes. Sew the ear or eye pieces together along the curved edge. Leave the straight edge open for turning right side out. Turn the pieces right side out and press them lightly.

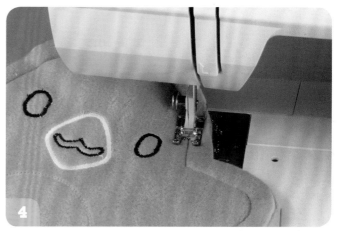

Sew the body pieces. Sew the puppet body front to the back along the curved edge. Insert the ears or frog eyes into the seam where the pattern guidelines indicate. Leave the bottom straight edge open for turning right side out. Clip the corners and curves and turn the puppet right side out. If using terrycloth, be sure to finish the edges as this fabric frays a lot when the edges are left unfinished.

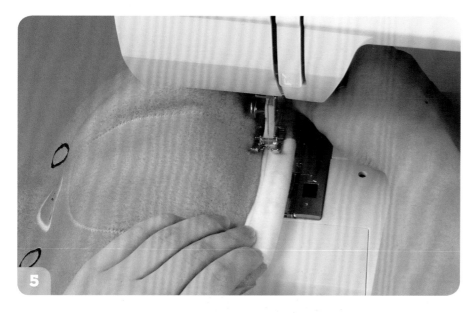

Hem the bottom. Make a double-fold hem along the bottom of the puppet. Fold under ⅝" (16mm) twice, then iron and sew the fold in place.

Fluffy Fat Plushies

LEVEL: **Easy**

Pattern on pages 116–118.

This chubby little guy isn't only made for babies, but he makes a great friend to your little one because he's big, round, and easy to hug. This will quickly be your baby's best pal to nap with, push around, or squeeze. The plush is best made with fleece or minky because the extra stretch from the fabric creates a nice smooth roundness. The pattern provides designs to make a pig, squirrel, or cat. It will be hard to resist making all three, either for yourself or to make a bold statement in any room where they're all assembled together.

Sew much more!

Swap out the face and ear patterns from the Body Pillows project (pages 123–126) for even more characters!

MATERIALS

- ⅔ yd (⅔m) of 60"-wide (1525mm) or 1 yd. (1m) of 45"-wide (1145mm) fleece or minky
- Thread to match fleece or minky fabrics
- Large bag of batting
- Appliqué fabrics
- Thread to match appliqué fabrics
- Fusible web
- Stabilizer

TOOLS

- Fabric marker
- Hand-sewing needle
- Fabric scissors
- Fabric pins

Variation: A true fat cat made using a textured fabric for baby's fingers to explore.

Variation: A stout and squishy squirrel!

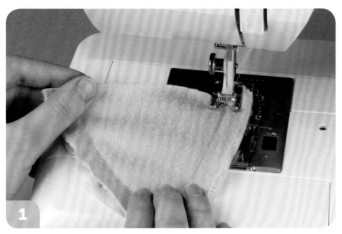

Sew all appendages. Sew the ears and tail for the character along the curved edge. Leave the straight edge open for turning right side out. Turn all pieces right side out and stuff the tail pieces with batting.

Sew the body quarters. Sew the body quarters along the long, slightly curved side to make two halves. Be sure to leave an opening in one half as indicated by the pattern for turning right side out.

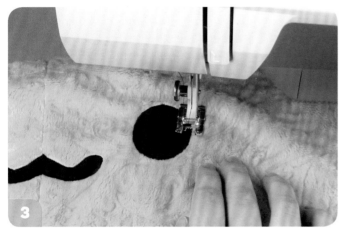

Appliqué the face. Cut and apply fusible web to the appliqué fabric. Iron and sew the appliqué pieces to the front half of the plush body. Place the appliqué pieces according to the pattern template, about 5″ (130mm) from the top of the body.

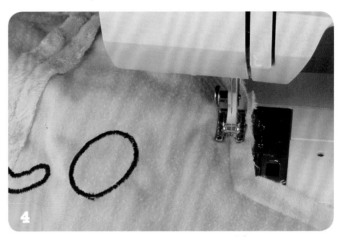

Sew the body front to the back. Sew the body front to the back, making sure to insert the ears as indicated by the pattern. Sew around all the edges and be sure to clip the corners and curves when complete.

Stuff and sew closed. Turn the body inside out and stuff tightly. Use a ladder stitch to hand-sew the opening closed in the back.

Attach tail. Fold under ⅝″ (16mm) of the tail opening and, using a ladder stitch, hand-sew it to the back of the animal body, about 5″ (130mm) from the bottom center seam. [For Squirrel: Hand-sew the top of the tail to the body so it stays upright and attached.] [For Pig: Twist the tail and hand-sew bits in place to keep it curled.]

Plush Fruit Cubes

LEVEL: Experienced Beginner

Pattern on page 119.

Alphabet blocks are a classic baby staple; for a fun twist, why not try fruit blocks? They're bright and the contrasting colors are sure to catch your baby's developing eyes. These are made to be just the right size for a baby to start learning to grab and stack things—an adorable way to work on those motor skills! You might have some fabric scraps from previous projects that can be put to good use here. The cubes use very little fabric and the color combinations are endless. Make one or make a basketful for lots of stacking and tumbling fun. The pattern includes pieces to make a lemon, watermelon, strawberry, and blueberries.

Sew much more!

If you still want to make traditional alphabet blocks, don't fret! Enlarge the monogram letters from the Plaid Quilt project (page 105) to 160% the size shown in the pattern section, and they should fit just fine on your squares.

MATERIALS

- ¼ yd. (¼m) or six 5" x 5" (130 x 130mm) scrap squares of various light- to medium-weight fabric

Appliqué fabric:
- Fat quarter of red cotton
- Fat quarter of green cotton
- Fat quarter of dark green cotton
- Fat quarter of white cotton
- Fat quarter of blue cotton
- Fat quarter of dark blue cotton
- Fat quarter of pink cotton
- Fat quarter of black cotton

- Thread to match appliqué fabric
- Thread to match main fabric
- Fusible web
- Stabilizer
- Batting

TOOLS

- Fabric scissors
- Fabric pins
- Fabric marker
- Hand-sewing needle
- Chopstick

Use this illustration as a guide for assembling your appliqué pieces into the different fruits.

Appliqué. Cut six 4¼" (110mm) squares from the main fabric. Cut out and apply fusible web to the appliqué fabric. Iron and sew it to the squares using the motif layout illustration as shown.

Chain the square pieces. Create a T shape with the squares: Using a ⅜" (10mm) seam allowance, sew a strip of four squares, then sew the last to the sides of the second square in the chain.

Sew the square sides. With right sides together, bring the squares surrounding the middle together along the edges. Sew them together to form the sides of the cube.

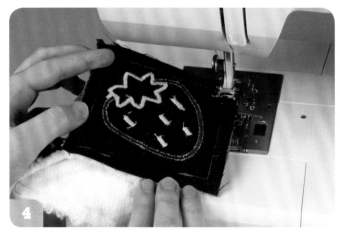

Sew the top. Bring the top piece down and sew to the sides, pivoting at the corners. Make sure to leave about 2" (50mm) open for turning the cube right side out.

Stuff and finish. Clip the corners of the cube and turn right side out. Poke the inside corners with a chopstick for a sharper definition. Stuff well with batting and hand-sew the opening closed with a ladder stitch.

Patchwork Plushies

LEVEL: Experienced Beginner

Pattern on pages 119–120.

Every little one needs a friend he can tote around. These little plush animals are perfect for the job. Being only lightly stuffed, they're great for easily grabbing and taking along on adventures. The real appeal to these little friends is that they're made with a variety of different fabrics to tantalize your baby's senses. Switch out the fabrics for the arms and legs with whatever great scraps you might have: satin, minky, corduroy, flannel, or plain cotton is fine. There's even an added pocket to hide a little surprise. All the tactile and visual variation is sure to keep your baby entertained. Best of all, there isn't too much hand-sewing involved in this project, so it will really stand up to all of the pulling, throwing, and grabbing that stuffed friends must endure. The pattern offers designs to make a koala, bat, or red panda.

Sew much more!

Swap out the face and ear patterns from the Hand Puppets project (pages 114–115) for even more characters!

MATERIALS

For Bat:
- ¼ yd. (¼m) purple fabric

For Koala:
- ¼ yd. (¼m) gray fabric
- ¼ yd. (¼m) or 12" x 12" (305 x 305mm) scrap of white fabric
- ⅛ yd. (⅛m) or 6" x 12" (150 x 305mm) scrap of long-pile faux fur or minky

For Red Panda:
- ¼ yd. (¼m) red fabric
- ⅛ yd. (⅛m) or 15" x 15" (380 x 380mm) scrap of black fabric

- *Optional:* Five 6" x 12" (150 x 305mm) scraps of various textured fabric for arms, legs, and pocket
- Thread to match main fabric
- Appliqué fabrics
- Thread to match appliqué fabric
- Batting
- Fusible web
- Stabilizer

TOOLS
- Fabric scissors
- Fabric pins
- Fabric marker
- Hand-sewing needle

← These adorable critters are perfect for naptime or playtime.

Sew the dart in the head front. Fold the head front piece in half and sew the dart at the top. Cut the dart open and press it flat.

Appliqué the face. Cut and iron fusible web to the appliqué fabric. Iron and sew the appliqué pieces to the face following the pattern guidelines.

For Tiger: Appliqué the tiger stripes. Sew the tiger stripes to the back of the body. Center them on the back piece about 6″ (150mm) and 12″ (305mm) from the tail end of the animal body.

Sew the ears and tail. [For Tiger: Sew tail tip to tail base and iron the seam flat.] Sew the ear and tail pieces together along the curved edge, leaving the straight edge open for turning right side out. Turn the pieces right side out. [For Bear: Hand-sew a running stitch along the outside of the tail circle. Gather the seam to make a sphere, stuffing lightly with batting. Cinch the seam and sew it closed.]

Sew the head. Sew the head front to the head back. Insert the ears in between using the guidelines from the pattern. Sew all the way around the head pieces. [For Tiger: Pinch the ears slightly while sewing the seam if desired.] Cut about a 5″ (130mm) vertical slit in the back of the head to turn it right side out. Stuff the head and whip stitch the opening closed.

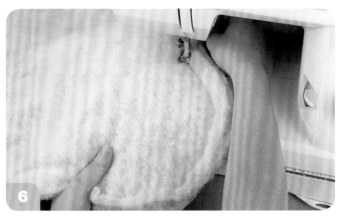

Sew the body pieces. Stack one layer of quilt batting, two fabric body pieces, right sides together, and the last layer of quilt batting (in that order). Sew the pieces together, leaving the opening as indicated by the circles in the pattern. Clip the convex and concave curves and turn the body inside out. Hand-sew the opening closed.

Sew the head to the body. Using a ladder stitch, hand-sew the animal head to the body between the arms at the front of the body. To ensure proper alignment, copy the circle marking to the body and back of the head. Mark notches at the four cardinal points for each circle and match them up as the head is sewn to the body.

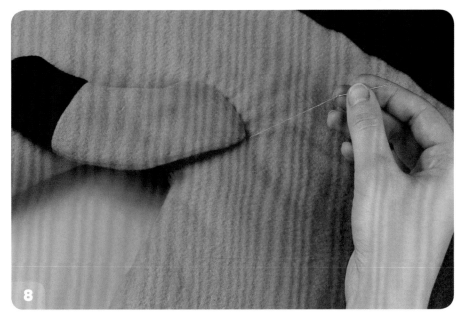

Sew the tail to the body. Turn under ⅝″ (16mm) of the tail piece, and, using a ladder stitch, hand-sew the tail piece to the body about 1½″–2½″ (40–65mm) from the tail end of the body.

practicalities

As much fun as it is to create adorable toys, clothes, and decorative projects, it helps to have some practical things around the house, too. With projects like the Petting Zoo Play Mat, an extremely cute Hooded Towel, or a Sleek Diaper Bag, you know you'll get exactly what you need and embellished just to your style. Also, projects like the Burp Cloths and Bibs use very little fabric, so stocking up on the essentials is easy and economical. Now even the routine baby items can have a fun twist.

The Petting Zoo Play Mat (page 92), Sleek Diaper Bag (page 96), and Ocean Bed Burp Cloths (page 84) are all charming practicalities you can really use! →

Ocean Bed Burp Cloths

LEVEL: Very Easy

Pattern on pages 127–128.

Baby items do not get more indispensible than burp cloths. While these are great to keep over your shoulder to catch little baby spills, they can easily work anywhere to do all kinds of cleaning and wiping. They're simple to make, so you can make a drawer full in a flash. You can then keep some in the bathroom, some in the nursery, some stashed by the changing table, and some in the kitchen for dinner time. Better yet, these are so sweet and colorful you'll want to keep them everywhere to brighten up any space. The simple burp cloth is made with cotton on one side and terry cloth on the other. The pattern includes designs to appliqué a trio of cute sea creatures: an octopus, squid, and whale.

Sew much more!

Swap out the appliqué patterns from the Plush Cubes project (page 119) for even more designs!

MATERIALS

- ½ yd. (½m) or a 14" x 14" (355 x 355mm) remnant of terry cloth
- ½ yd. (½m) or a 14" x 14" (355 x 355mm) remnant of cotton
- Thread to match main fabric
- Appliqué fabrics
- Thread to match appliqué fabric
- Fusible web
- Stabilizer

TOOLS

- Fabric scissors
- Fabric pins
- Fabric marker
- Hand-sewing needle

1

Appliqué the characters. Cut and apply fusible web to the appliqué fabric. Iron and sew the appliqué pieces to the bottom corner of the cotton piece following the pattern guidelines.

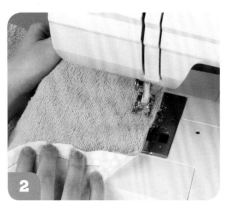

2

Sew the body of the cloth. Sew the wrong side of the terry cloth piece to the wrong side of the cotton piece all along the edge, leaving an opening where indicated by the pattern to turn right side out. Turn the towel right side out and press.

3

Sew the opening closed. Using a ladder stitch, hand-sew the opening closed on the side of the cloth.

Cuddly Creatures Hooded Towel

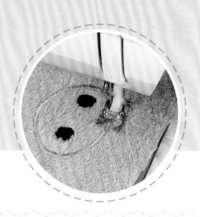

LEVEL: Easy

Pattern on pages 129–132.

This adorable towel might become your baby's favorite item of all, and definitely makes bath time a lot more fun. The large hood means that it will still fit your baby just fine years down the road. The towel itself is very wide, making it easy to snuggly wrap up your baby right out of the bath. Make this with fluffy terry cloth fabric or use a cut-up towel. In fact, if you line up the corners of the pattern with the finished edges of the towel, you can skip hemming or finishing seams. Cut-up terry cloth can unravel quite a bit, so be sure to finish the raw edges whenever possible. The pattern comes with designs to make an otter, frog, or pig.

Sew much more!

Swap out the face and ear patterns from the Bibs (pages 132–133), Character Hats (pages 106–109), or Bloomers (page 113) projects for even more characters!

MATERIALS

- 1½ yds. (1½m) terry cloth or 1 bath towel and 1 hand towel
- Thread to match main fabric
- Appliqué fabric
- Thread to match appliqué fabric
- Fusible web
- Stabilizer

TOOLS

- Fabric scissors
- Fabric pins
- Fabric marker

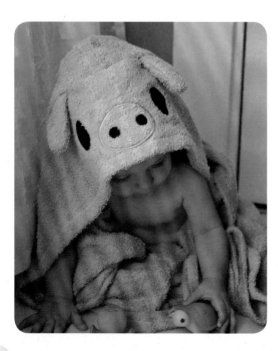

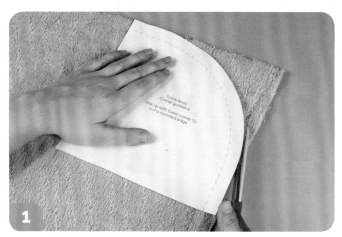

Trim the main towel. Cut a 32″ x 48″ (815 x 1220mm) square of terry cloth. Using the pattern guideline, trim the fabric so each corner is rounded.

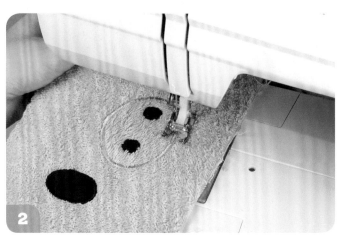

Appliqué the face. Cut and apply fusible web to the appliqué fabric. Iron and sew the appliqué pieces to the hood front along the pattern guideline. [For Frog: Also appliqué the frog pupil to the frog eye.]

Sew the ears and eyes. Sew the ear and eye pieces together along the curved edge, leaving the straight edge open for turning right side out. Turn the pieces right side out.

Sew the hood back. Sew the hood back pieces together along the curved edge, leaving the bottom and straight (front) edge open.

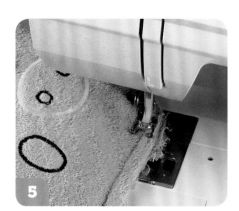

Sew the hood front to the back. Sew the hood front to the hood back along the shorter of the two straight edges. Insert the ears or eyes into the seam as indicated by the pattern.

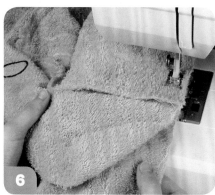

Sew the hood to the main towel. Find the center of the long side of the main towel. Match this up with the center of the hood and sew them together. Start ⅝″ (16mm) from the beginning edge and finish ⅝″ (16mm) away from the end.

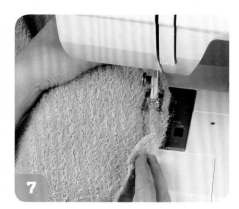

Hem the outside edges. Fold under the outer edges of the hood and main towel piece by ⅝″ (16mm). Iron the fold in place and hem the fabric, using a medium zigzag stitch that overlaps the raw edge of the fabric. This will both hem the fabric and finish the raw edge to prevent any unraveling.

Cottony Clean Bibs

LEVEL: **Easy**

Pattern on pages 132–133.

You can keep your baby's face nice and clean with this useful bib. Not only does it make feeding time cheery, but it doubles as a cleaning cloth because the underside is made with absorbent terry cloth. It's easy to get the bib on and off—with tabs of hook-and-loop tape, there's no fuss in getting your baby ready for dinnertime. Less than a yard of fabric can make a decent amount of bibs, so you can make plenty to be ready for whatever spills come. The pattern comes with designs to make a monkey, pig, and mouse.

Sew much more!

Swap out the face and ear patterns from the Hooded Towels (page 129), Character Hats (pages 106–109), or Bloomers (page 13) projects for even more characters!

MATERIALS

- ½ yd. (½m) cotton
- *Additional for Monkey:* ¼ yd. (¼m) contrast cotton for face and ears
- ½ yd. (½m) terry cloth
- 1" (25mm) of ¾" (19mm) hook-and-loop tape
- Thread to match main fabrics
- Appliqué fabrics
- Thread to match appliqué fabrics
- Fusible web
- Stabilizer

TOOLS

- Fabric scissors
- Fabric pins
- Fabric marker

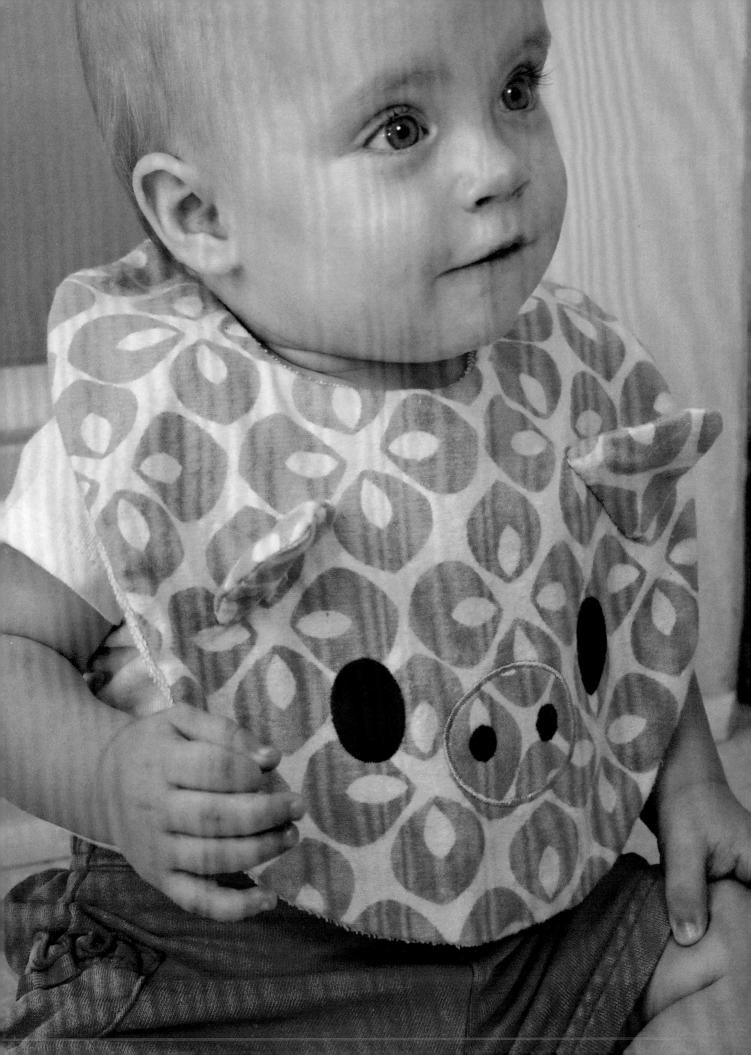

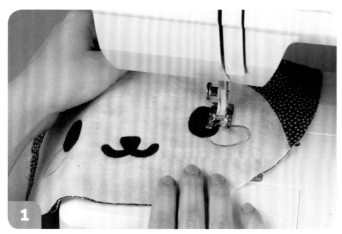

Appliqué the faces. Cut and apply fusible web to the appliqué fabric. Iron and sew the appliqué pieces to the bib front as indicated by the pattern guidelines.

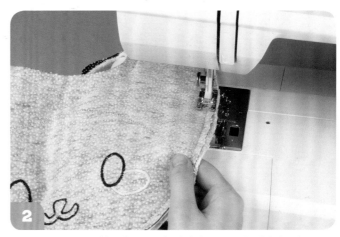

Sew the front and back. Sew the bib front to the bib back around the entire edge. Be sure to leave an opening where the pattern indicates for turning right side out. Clip the curves of the bib, turn it right side out, and press it.

Sew the opening closed. Using a ladder stitch, hand-sew the opening of the bib closed.

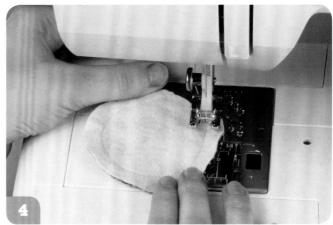

Sew the ears. Sew the ear pieces along the curved edge. Leave the straight edge open for turning right side out. Turn the ears right side out, turn under the opening by ⅜″ (10mm), and press them.

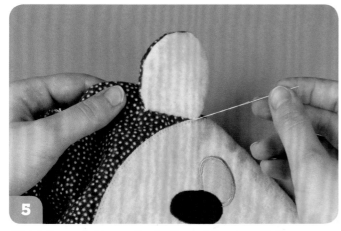

Attach the ears. Line up the bottom of the ear with the guideline on the pattern and hand-sew it to the front of the bib.

Attach the hook and loop tape. Following the pattern guidelines, place the hook-and-loop tape on the tabs of the bib. Sew the hook side on the bottom of the left tab, and the loop side on the top of the right tab.

Petting Zoo Play Mat

LEVEL: Experienced Beginner

Pattern on pages 134–135.

This adorable and fuzzy play mat is useful in so many ways. Not only is it cozy and plush to sit on, but it's also covered in appliquéd animals made from super-soft minky that are impossible not to touch. Your baby can have fun petting them until he or she gets older and can learn to name the animals and match up the pairs. It's perfect for your baby just to lounge on or as a wall hanging or lap quilt. The simple checker design can be done in a number of colors, from sweet and understated to wild and bold. The finished size is 40" x 40" (1015 x 1015mm), and the pattern includes designs to make a kitty, bunny, elephant, llama, and sheep appliqué.

MATERIALS

- ⅓ yd. (⅓m) of cotton in Color A
- ⅓ yd. (⅓m) of cotton in Color B
- ⅓ yd. (⅓m) of cotton in Color C
- ⅓ yd. (⅓m) of cotton in Color D
- ⅓ yd. (⅓m) of cotton in Color E
- 1¼ yd. (1¼m) of cotton for borders
- 1¼ yd. (1¼m) of cotton for backing
- 1⅓ yd. (1⅓m) of cotton for binding
- 44" x 44" (1120 x 1120mm) of quilt batting

Appliqué fabrics:

- ¼ yd (¼m) or 9" x 18" (230 x 460mm) remnant of gray minky
- ¼ yd (¼m) or 9" x 18" (230 x 460mm) remnant of white minky
- ¼ yd (¼m) or 9" x 18" (230 x 460mm) remnant of blue minky
- ¼ yd (¼m) or 9" x 18" (230 x 460mm) remnant of purple or pink minky
- ¼ yd (¼m) or 9" x 18" (230 x 460mm) remnant of green minky
- Fat quarter of cream cotton
- Fat quarter of black cotton

- Thread to match main fabrics
- Thread to match appliqué fabrics
- Fusible web
- Stabilizer

TOOLS

- Fabric scissors
- Fabric pins
- Fabric marker
- Safety pins

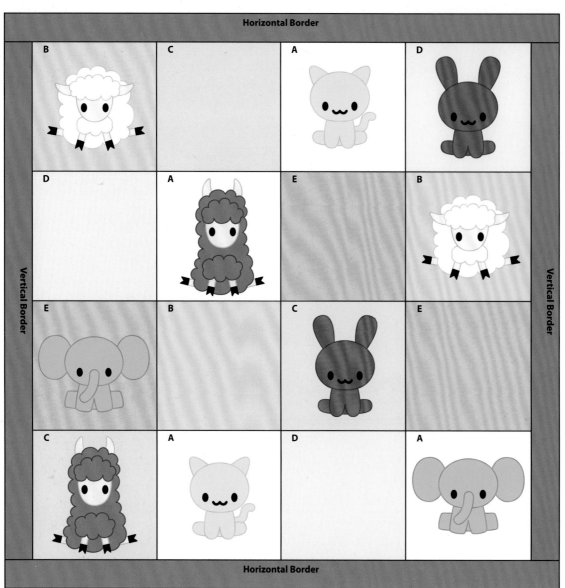

Use this illustration to assemble your
colored quilt squares in the right order.

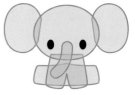

Cut the various rectangle and square pieces from the fabric following the chart below:

Fabric Color	Size to Cut	Number to Cut	Seam Allowance
A	9½" x 9½" (240 x 240mm)	4	¼ " (6mm)
B	9½" x 9½" (240 x 240mm)	3	¼" (6mm)
C	9½" x 9½" (240 x 240mm)	3	¼" (6mm)
D	9½" x 9½" (240 x 240mm)	3	¼" (6mm)
E	9½" x 9½" (240 x 240mm)	3	¼" (6mm)
Vertical Border	2¼ " x 36" (60 x 915mm)	2	¼" (6mm)
Horizontal Border	2¼" x 40" (60 x 1015mm)	2	¼" (6mm)
Binding	3½" x 48" (90 x 1220mm)	4	½" (13mm)

Use this illustration
to assemble
your appliqué
pieces to make
the characters.

1

Appliqué the characters. Cut and apply fusible web to the appliqué fabric. Using the character layout illustration, arrange the appliqué pieces. Iron and sew the appliqué pieces to the corresponding quilt square.

2

Sew the rows of blocks. Following the illustration, sew the rows of various color blocks. Create a row of colors B, C, A, and D. Then create a row of colors D, A, E, and B. Then create a row of E, B, C, and E. Then, lastly, make a row of C, A, D, and A. Include the appliquéd blocks where indicated by the illustration.

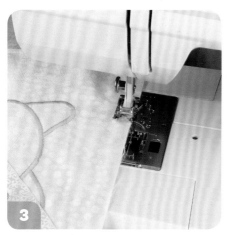

3

Sew the rows together. Sew the rows along their long sides following the quilt layout illustration. This will create a complete 4-block by 4-block square.

4

Sew the side borders. Sew the vertical border pieces to the sides of the quilt square.

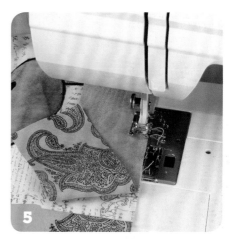

5

Sew the top and bottom borders. Sew the horizontal border pieces to the top and bottom of the quilt.

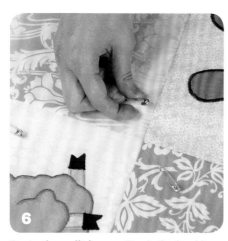

6

Baste the quilt layers. Stack the backing fabric, quilt batting, and quilt top (in that order) on a large flat surface. Smooth out as many wrinkles as possible and, working outward from the middle, begin pinning the layers together with safety pins every 5"–10" (130–255mm).

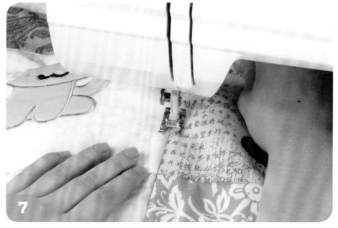

7

Quilt the layers. With a slightly longer straight stitch, sew through all the layers of the quilt along the edges of the blocks. Work from the center outward and smooth the fabric constantly, making sure all the layers are perfectly even. When it's complete, trim the excess quilt batting and backing sticking out from the quilt top.

8

Bind the quilt. Use the guide for "Binding a Quilt" (page 34) to finish the quilt.

Sleek Diaper Bag

LEVEL: Intermediate

Pattern on pages 135–141.

This bag is for all those busy yet stylish moms and dads out there. It was designed for holding just a few essentials, like diapers, a bottle, wipes, and a couple of other necessities. The sash-like shape means that your arms are free to hold onto your baby or anything else important. Either way, it works wonderfully for parents who are doing a quick errand and don't need to bring everything but the kitchen sink—or perhaps you are toilet training a toddler and only need something in case of emergencies. The construction has a few more steps than most because the bag is loaded with useful pockets, but it's definitely worth it when you see all it can hold. With that in mind, try to pick a good sturdy fabric such as canvas or twill. The pattern comes with designs for an optional Super Dad, Super Mom, or Baby Jolly Roger appliqué, and it also varies between extra small and extra large sizes to accommodate parents of nearly all sizes.

MATERIALS
- 1 yd. (1m) canvas or twill fabric
- 1 yd. (1m) of ¾" (19mm)-wide hook-and-loop tape
- ½ yd. (½m) of ¼" (6mm)-wide elastic
- Thread to match fabric
- Appliqué fabric (optional)
- Thread to match appliqué fabric (optional)
- Fusible web (optional)
- Stabilizer (optional)

TOOLS
- Fabric marker
- Fabric scissors
- Fabric pins

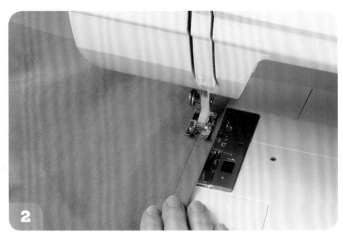

Prepare the pocket seam allowances. Prepare the side, flat, and deep pockets. Turn under ⅝" (16mm) on the left edge of the side pocket (D), and the bottom edge of two of the deep pockets (G and H) and the flat pocket (E). Iron these folds in place to prepare for the next steps.

Hem the pocket top edges. Turn under ⅝" (16mm) of the top of each pocket (D–H) and hem the fold in place.

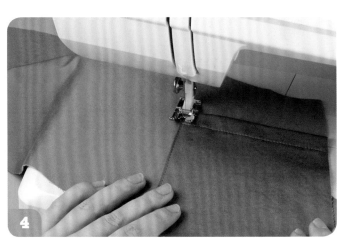

Appliqué the flat pocket (optional). Cut out and apply fusible web to the appliqué pieces. Iron and sew the appliqué pieces to the flat pocket (E), centering in the middle of the pocket.

Apply the side pocket. Line up the side pocket (D) to the side front piece. Sew the pocket in place along the left edge.

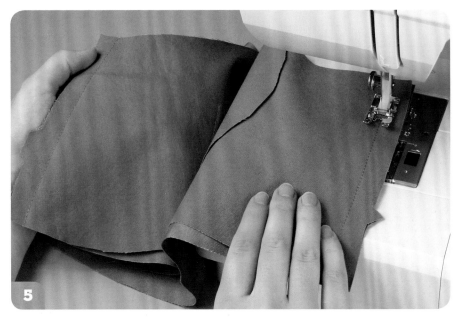

The diaper bag is essentially a sash with attached pockets that wraps around the body and is secured with hook-and-loop tape.

Sew the main bag pieces. Sew the bag front (A) to the bag middle (C), matching the single notches. Sew the bag side (B) to the bag middle (C), matching the double notches. Do this with the other set of pieces to create the bag underside and outside.

Sew the pocket flap. Sew the pocket flap pieces (I) together, leaving the top long edge open for turning right side out. Clip the corners and turn right side out, then press.

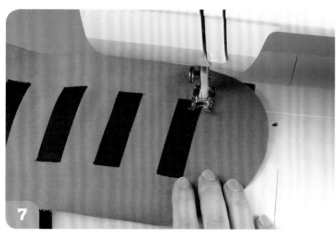

Apply the hook-and-loop tape. Using the pattern guidelines, sew hook-and-loop tape to the areas indicated. Sew 2" (50mm) pieces to the pocket flap and one deep pocket piece. Also apply 3" (75mm) to the bag underside (the side that does not have the side pocket [D]) and 6" (150mm) pieces to the bag outside (the side that has the side pocket attached).

Add elastic to the deep pockets. Thread a 6¼" (160mm) piece of elastic through the top hem of two of the deep pockets (F and G). Sew a few stitches to anchor the elastic on each side of the pocket to create a gathered effect.

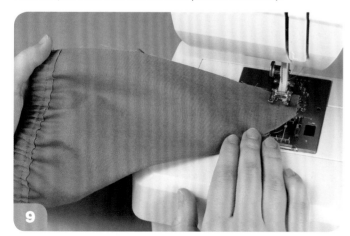

Sew the deep pocket corners. Fold the corners of the deep pockets (F–H) at 45° angles to make the edges match. Note that if the pocket has a turned under bottom side (G and H), the bottom edges will not match up. Sew them together then cut and press open the seam allowances.

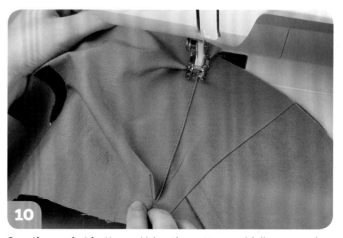

Sew the pocket bottoms. Using the pattern guidelines, sew the flat pocket (E) to the bag front (A) along the bottom edge. Do this also on the bag middle with one elastic pocket (G) on top and the hook-and-loop tape pocket (H) on bottom.

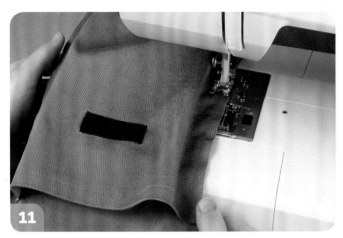

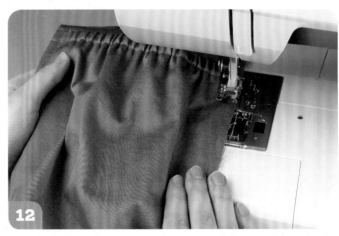

Baste the pocket sides. Baste the sides of the attached pockets (E, G, and H) within the ⅝" (16mm) seam allowance so that they do not shift while the rest of the bag is sewn.

Sew the end pocket. Line up the edges of the remaining elastic pocket (F) to the end of the bag front. Use the guideline from the pattern to make sure the edges line up evenly.

Sew the pocket flap. With right sides together, sew the pocket flap (I) along the guideline above the pocket (H). Fold the flap down and sew it again about ¼" (6mm) from the seam to hold it in place.

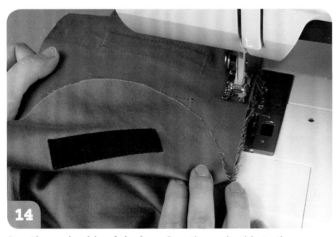

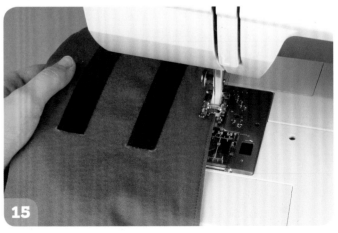

Sew the underside of the bag. Sew the underside to the outside of the bag along the edges, leaving an opening as indicated by the pattern to turn right side out. Be sure not to catch any of the extra pocket fabric.

Turn and finish the bag. Turn the bag right side out and press. Turn under the opening left and machine-sew it closed, close to the edge of the bag.

patterns

This section contains all of the pattern pieces you'll need to create the projects in the front part of the book. Photocopy all the necessary pieces at 150% (except for Plaid Quilt pattern, page 105) and get sewing!

Floating Friends Mobiles
pages 20–23

Owls

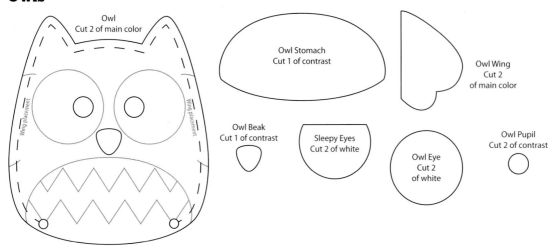

Owl
Cut 2 of main color

Wing placement

Wing placement

Owl Stomach
Cut 1 of contrast

Owl Wing
Cut 2
of main color

Owl Beak
Cut 1 of contrast

Sleepy Eyes
Cut 2 of white

Owl Eye
Cut 2
of white

Owl Pupil
Cut 2 of contrast

Robots

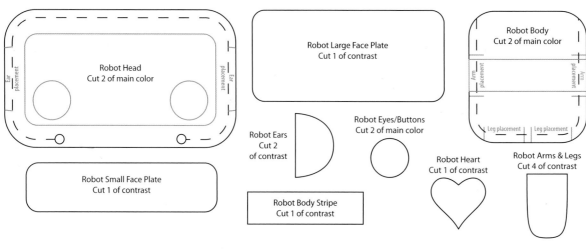

Ear placement

Robot Head
Cut 2 of main color

Ear placement

Robot Large Face Plate
Cut 1 of contrast

Robot Body
Cut 2 of main color

Arm placement

Arm placement

Leg placement

Leg placement

Robot Eyes/Buttons
Cut 2 of main color

Robot Ears
Cut 2
of contrast

Robot Heart
Cut 1 of contrast

Robot Arms & Legs
Cut 4 of contrast

Robot Small Face Plate
Cut 1 of contrast

Robot Body Stripe
Cut 1 of contrast

Storm Clouds

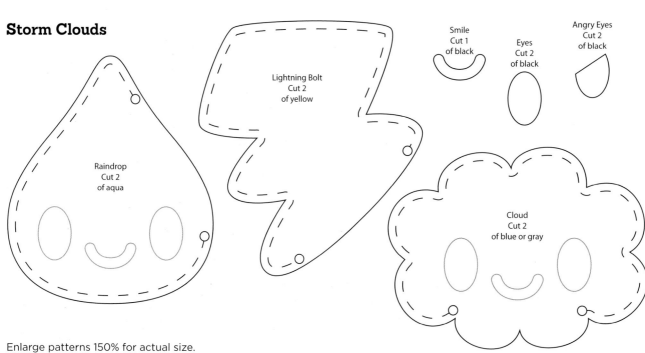

Lightning Bolt
Cut 2
of yellow

Smile
Cut 1
of black

Eyes
Cut 2
of black

Angry Eyes
Cut 2
of black

Raindrop
Cut 2
of aqua

Cloud
Cut 2
of blue or gray

Enlarge patterns 150% for actual size.

Pirate Isle Toy Organizer
pages 24–28

Pirate Kitty

Head
Cut 1 of red

Hilt
Cut 1 of brown

Eyepatch Strap
Cut 1 of black

Eye
Cut 1 of black

Body
Cut 1 of red

Smile
Cut 1 of black

Eyepatch
Cut 1 of black

Ear
Cut 2 of red

Tail
Cut 1 of red

Left Hand
Cut 1 of red

Right Arm
Cut 1 of red

Cutlass
Cut 1 of gray

Left Arm
Cut 1 of red

Legs
Cut 2 of red

Pirate Ship

Sail 1
Cut 1 of white

Sail 2
Cut 1 of white

Sail 4
Cut 1 of white

Sail 3
Cut 1 of white

Jolly Roger
Cut 1 of black

Mast 2
Cut 1 of brown

Flag
Cut 1 of red

Inner ship
Cut 1 of dark brown

Outer Ship
Cut 1 of brown

Mast 1
Cut 1 of brown

Mast 3
Cut 1 of brown

Pirate Panda

Bandana
Cut 1 of red

Right Leg
Cut 1 of black

Body
Cut 1 of white

Head
Cut 1 of white

Telescope 1
Cut 1 of brown

Telescope 2
Cut 1 of dark brown

Bandana Knot 1
Cut 1 of red

Telescope 3
Cut 1 of black

Bandana Knot 2
Cut 1 of red

Eye
Cut 1 of black

Ears
Cut 2 of black

Left Leg
Cut 1 of black

Arms
Cut 2 of black

Bandana Knot 3
Cut 1 of red

Stone
Cut 1 of gray

Tail
Cut 1 of black

Smile
Cut 1 of black

Enlarge patterns 150% for actual size.

Pirate Isle Toy Organizer (continued)

Mermaid Bunny

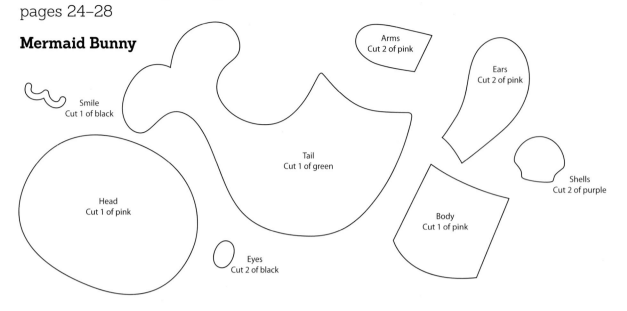

Smile
Cut 1 of black

Arms
Cut 2 of pink

Ears
Cut 2 of pink

Tail
Cut 1 of green

Head
Cut 1 of pink

Body
Cut 1 of pink

Shells
Cut 2 of purple

Eyes
Cut 2 of black

Treasure Chest

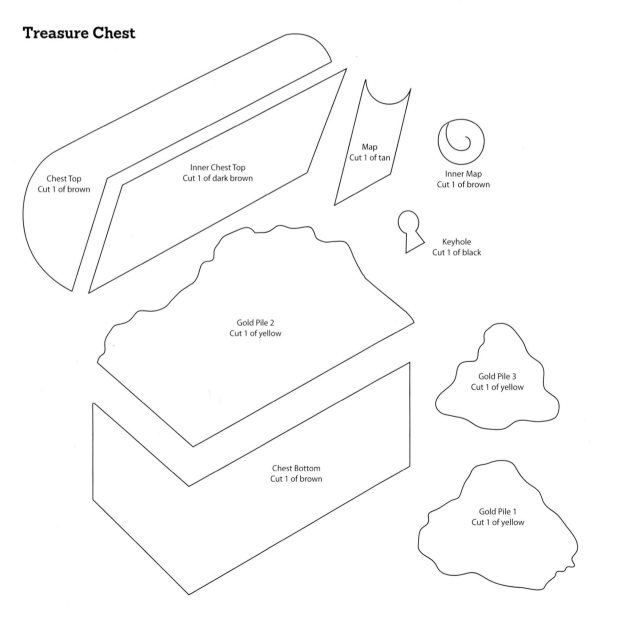

Chest Top
Cut 1 of brown

Inner Chest Top
Cut 1 of dark brown

Map
Cut 1 of tan

Inner Map
Cut 1 of brown

Keyhole
Cut 1 of black

Gold Pile 2
Cut 1 of yellow

Gold Pile 3
Cut 1 of yellow

Chest Bottom
Cut 1 of brown

Gold Pile 1
Cut 1 of yellow

Enlarge patterns 150% for actual size.

Plaid and Argyle Quilt

pages 29–39

Enlarge patterns 650% for actual size.

Fuzzy Menagerie Character Hats

pages 42–47

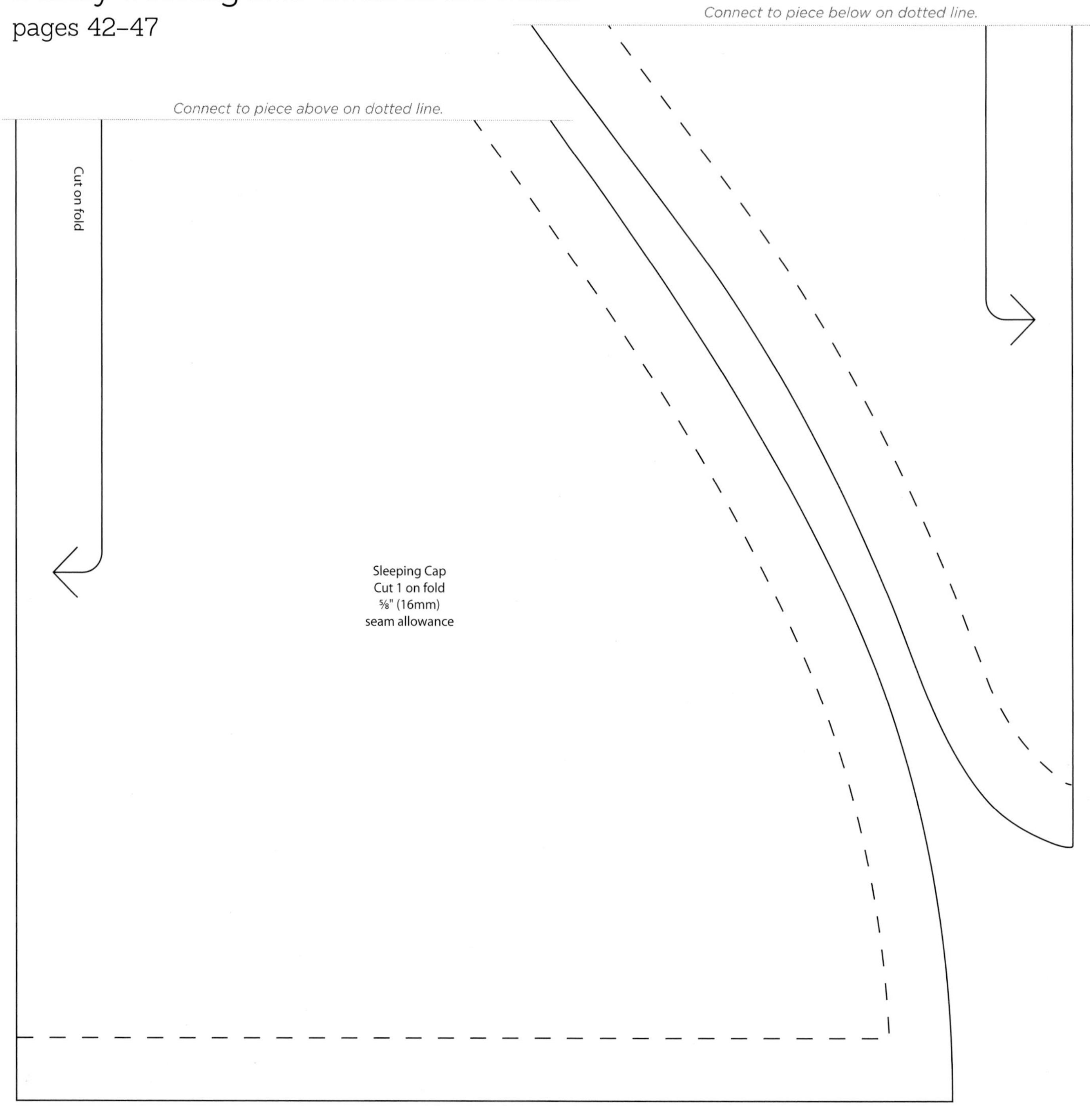

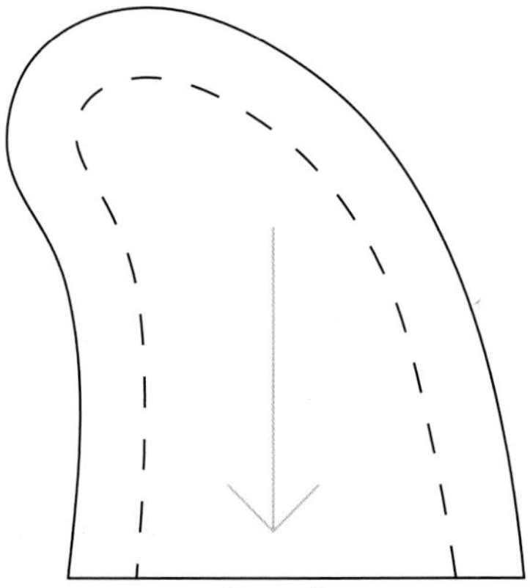

Connect to piece above on dotted line.

Connect to piece below on dotted line.

Cut on fold

Sleeping Cap
Cut 1 on fold
⅝" (16mm)
seam allowance

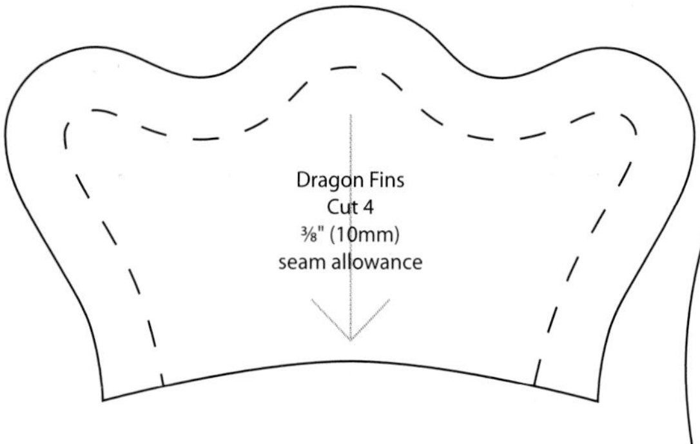

Dragon Fins
Cut 4
⅜" (10mm)
seam allowance

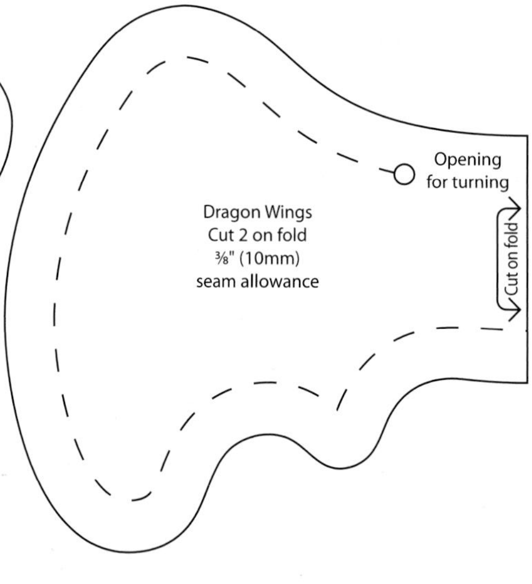

Dragon Wings
Cut 2 on fold
⅜" (10mm)
seam allowance

Opening
for turning

Cut on fold

Dragon Horns
Cut 4 of contrast color
⅜" (10mm)
seam allowance

Enlarge patterns 150% for actual size.

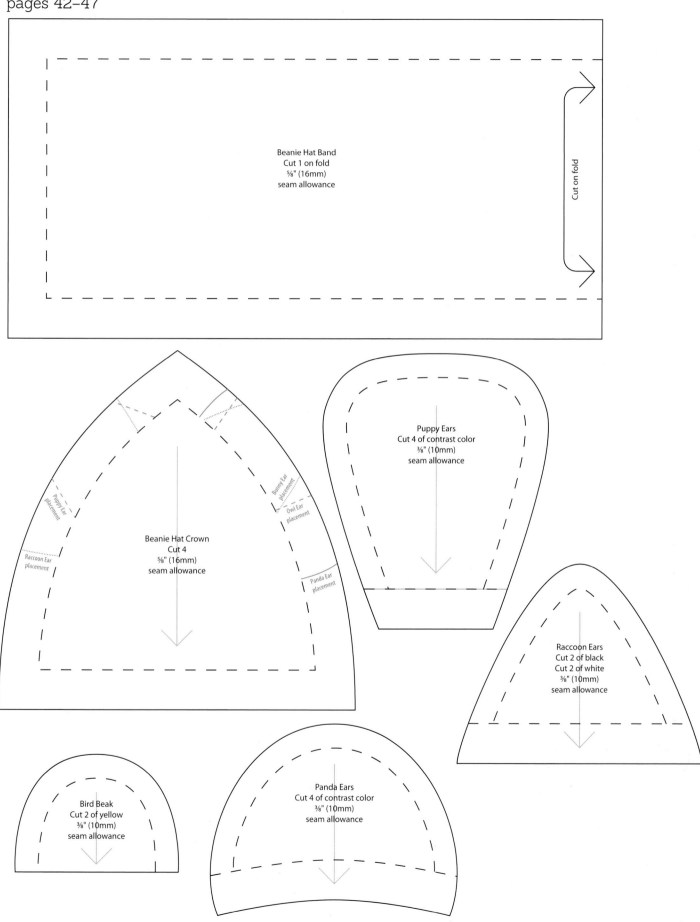

Beanie Hat Band
Cut 1 on fold
⅝" (16mm)
seam allowance

Cut on fold

Puppy Ears
Cut 4 of contrast color
⅜" (10mm)
seam allowance

Bunny Ear placement

Owl Ear placement

Puppy Ear placement

Raccoon Ear placement

Beanie Hat Crown
Cut 4
⅝" (16mm)
seam allowance

Panda Ear placement

Raccoon Ears
Cut 2 of black
Cut 2 of white
⅜" (10mm)
seam allowance

Bird Beak
Cut 2 of yellow
⅜" (10mm)
seam allowance

Panda Ears
Cut 4 of contrast color
⅜" (10mm)
seam allowance

Enlarge patterns 150% for actual size.

Fuzzy Menagerie Character Hats (continued)

pages 42–47

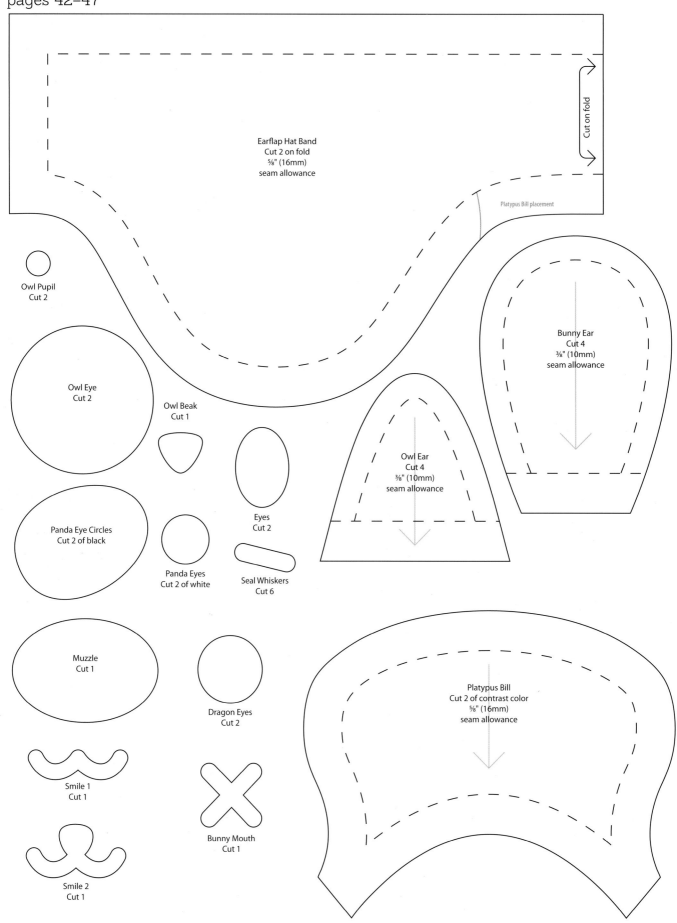

Earflap Hat Band
Cut 2 on fold
⅝" (16mm)
seam allowance

Cut on fold

Platypus Bill placement

Owl Pupil
Cut 2

Bunny Ear
Cut 4
⅜" (10mm)
seam allowance

Owl Eye
Cut 2

Owl Beak
Cut 1

Eyes
Cut 2

Owl Ear
Cut 4
⅜" (10mm)
seam allowance

Panda Eye Circles
Cut 2 of black

Panda Eyes
Cut 2 of white

Seal Whiskers
Cut 6

Muzzle
Cut 1

Dragon Eyes
Cut 2

Platypus Bill
Cut 2 of contrast color
⅝" (16mm)
seam allowance

Smile 1
Cut 1

Bunny Mouth
Cut 1

Smile 2
Cut 1

Enlarge patterns 150% for actual size.

Fuzzy Menagerie Character Hats (continued)
pages 42–47

Puppy Face

Bunny Face

Raccoon Face

Panda Face

Dragon Face

Owl Face

Seal Face

Platypus Face

Bird Face

Beak
placement

Enlarge patterns 150% for actual size.

Chinese Zodiac Headbands

pages 48–53

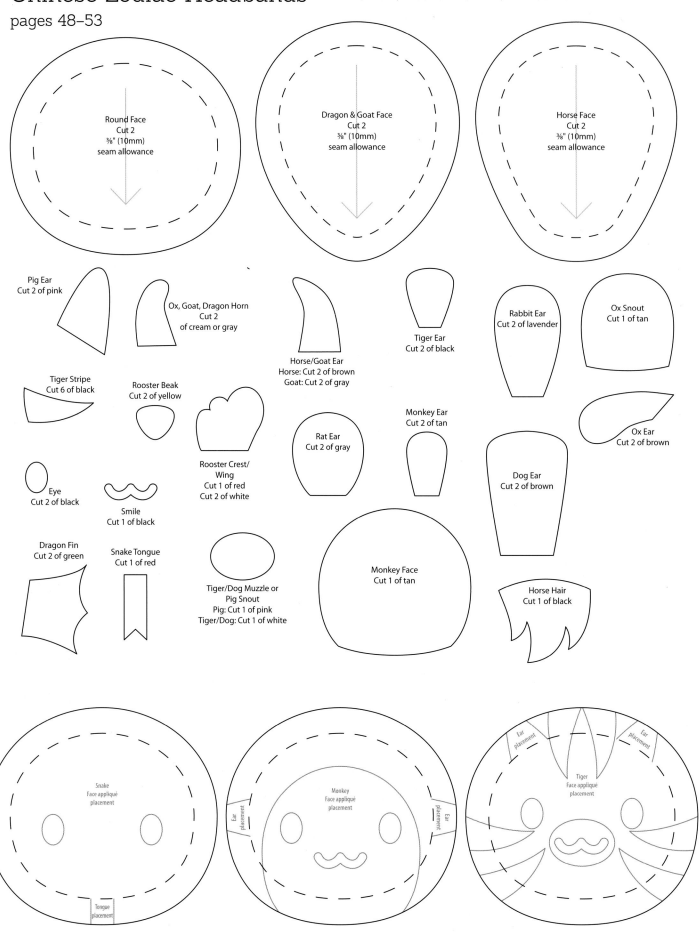

Round Face
Cut 2
⅜" (10mm)
seam allowance

Dragon & Goat Face
Cut 2
⅜" (10mm)
seam allowance

Horse Face
Cut 2
⅜" (10mm)
seam allowance

Pig Ear
Cut 2 of pink

Ox, Goat, Dragon Horn
Cut 2
of cream or gray

Horse/Goat Ear
Horse: Cut 2 of brown
Goat: Cut 2 of gray

Tiger Ear
Cut 2 of black

Rabbit Ear
Cut 2 of lavender

Ox Snout
Cut 1 of tan

Tiger Stripe
Cut 6 of black

Rooster Beak
Cut 2 of yellow

Rat Ear
Cut 2 of gray

Monkey Ear
Cut 2 of tan

Ox Ear
Cut 2 of brown

Eye
Cut 2 of black

Smile
Cut 1 of black

Rooster Crest/
Wing
Cut 1 of red
Cut 2 of white

Dog Ear
Cut 2 of brown

Dragon Fin
Cut 2 of green

Snake Tongue
Cut 1 of red

Tiger/Dog Muzzle or
Pig Snout
Pig: Cut 1 of pink
Tiger/Dog: Cut 1 of white

Monkey Face
Cut 1 of tan

Horse Hair
Cut 1 of black

Snake
Face appliqué
placement

Tongue
placement

Monkey
Face appliqué
placement

Ear
placement

Ear
placement

Ear
placement

Ear
placement

Tiger
Face appliqué
placement

Enlarge patterns 150% for actual size.

Chinese Zodiac Headbands (continued)
pages 48–53

Enlarge patterns 150% for actual size.

Cozy Critters Baby Booties

pages 54–56

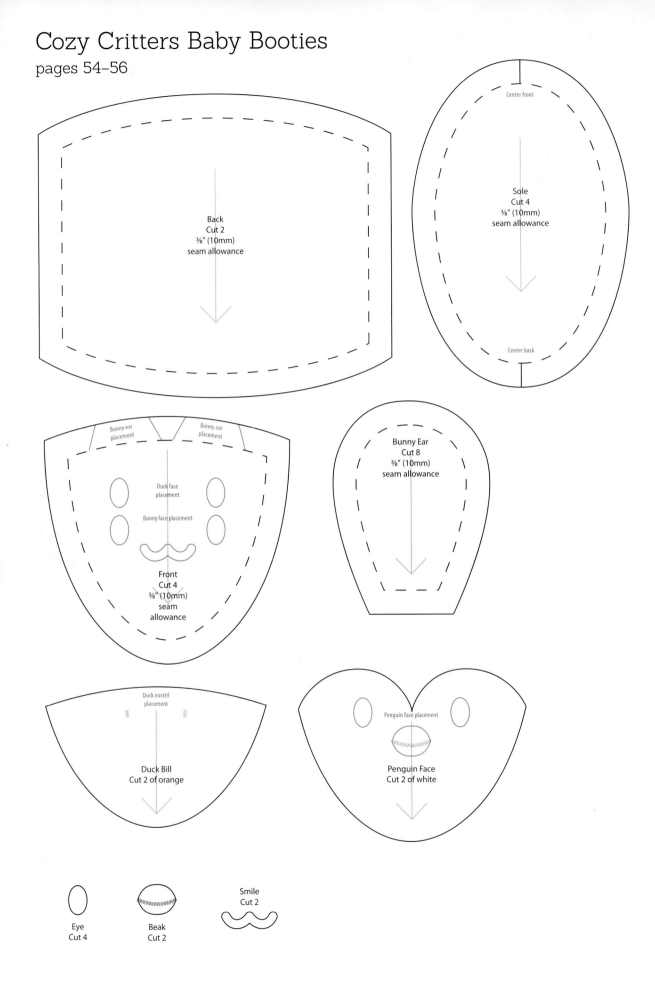

Back
Cut 2
⅜" (10mm)
seam allowance

Sole
Cut 4
⅜" (10mm)
seam allowance

Center front

Center back

Bunny ear placement

Bunny ear placement

Duck face placement

Bunny face placement

Front
Cut 4
⅜" (10mm)
seam allowance

Bunny Ear
Cut 8
⅜" (10mm)
seam allowance

Duck nostril placement

Duck Bill
Cut 2 of orange

Penguin face placement

Penguin Face
Cut 2 of white

Eye
Cut 4

Beak
Cut 2

Smile
Cut 2

Enlarge patterns 150% for actual size.

Sweet Bottoms Baby Bloomers

pages 57–59

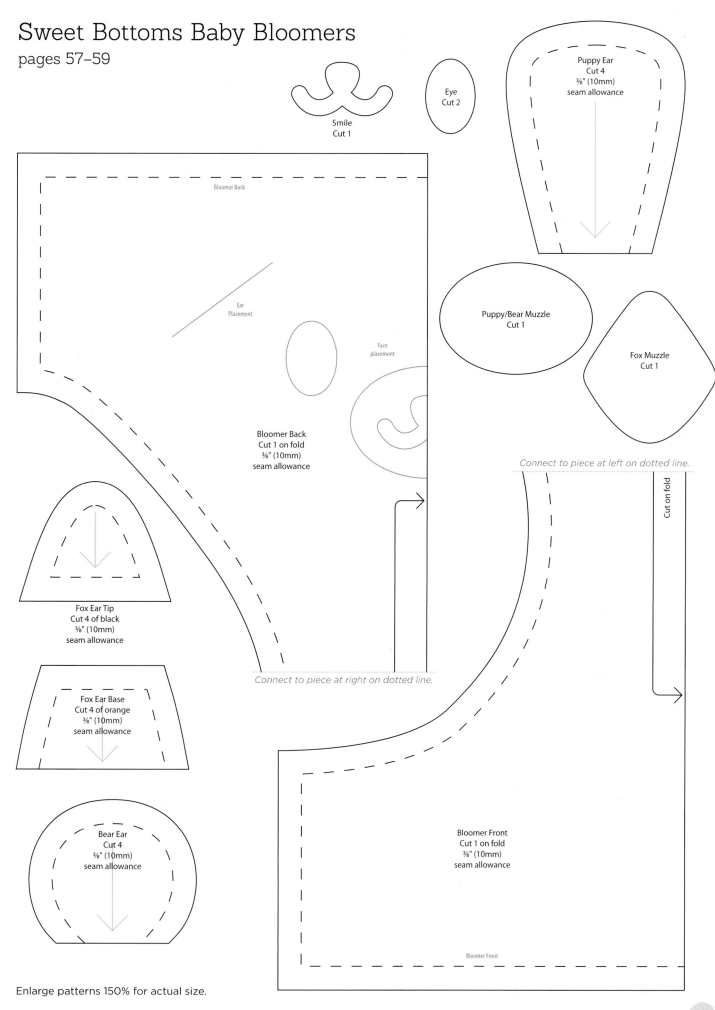

Smile
Cut 1

Eye
Cut 2

Puppy Ear
Cut 4
⅜" (10mm)
seam allowance

Bloomer Back

Ear
Placement

Face
placement

Puppy/Bear Muzzle
Cut 1

Fox Muzzle
Cut 1

Bloomer Back
Cut 1 on fold
⅜" (10mm)
seam allowance

Connect to piece at left on dotted line.

Cut on fold

Fox Ear Tip
Cut 4 of black
⅜" (10mm)
seam allowance

Connect to piece at right on dotted line.

Fox Ear Base
Cut 4 of orange
⅜" (10mm)
seam allowance

Bloomer Front
Cut 1 on fold
⅜" (10mm)
seam allowance

Bear Ear
Cut 4
⅜" (10mm)
seam allowance

Bloomer Front

Enlarge patterns 150% for actual size.

Forest Friends Hand Puppets
pages 62–65

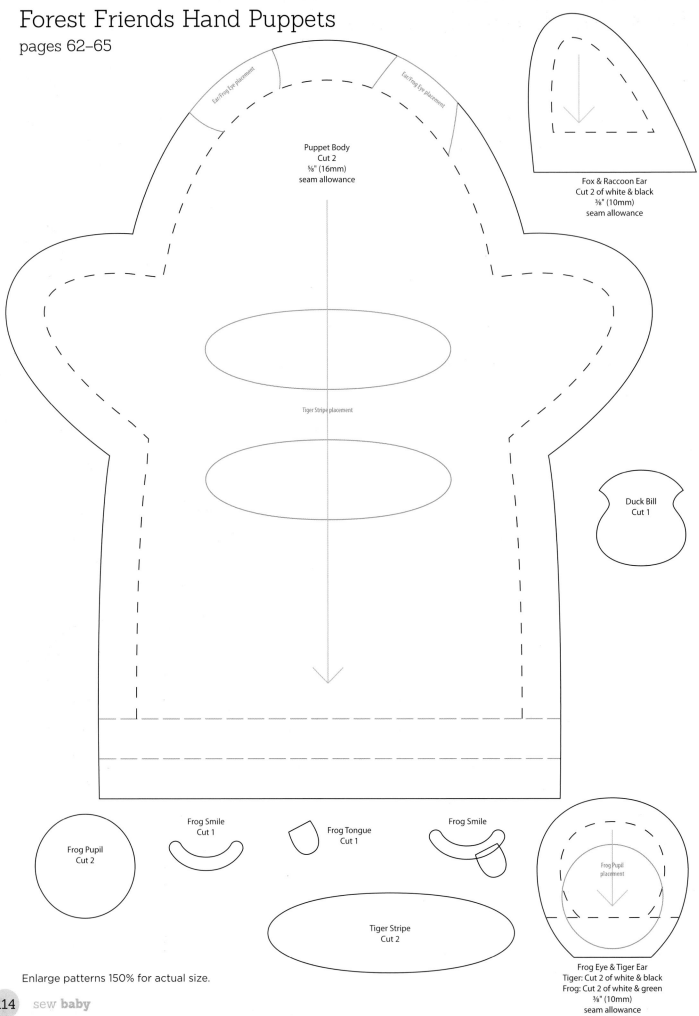

Puppet Body
Cut 2
⅝" (16mm)
seam allowance

Ear/Frog Eye placement

Ear/Frog Eye placement

Tiger Stripe placement

Fox & Raccoon Ear
Cut 2 of white & black
⅜" (10mm)
seam allowance

Duck Bill
Cut 1

Frog Pupil
Cut 2

Frog Smile
Cut 1

Frog Tongue
Cut 1

Frog Smile

Tiger Stripe
Cut 2

Frog Pupil
placement

Frog Eye & Tiger Ear
Tiger: Cut 2 of white & black
Frog: Cut 2 of white & green
⅜" (10mm)
seam allowance

Enlarge patterns 150% for actual size.

Forest Friends Hand Puppets (continued)
pages 62–65

Raccoon Face

Fox Face

Penguin Face

Tiger Face

Duck Face

Muzzle
Cut 1

Smile
Cut 1

Penguin Beak
Cut 1

Eye
Cut 2

Penguin Stomach
Cut 1 of white

Fox, Raccoon & Tiger Stomach
Cut 1 of white

Raccoon Eye Marking
Cut 2

Raccoon Eye
Cut 2

Enlarge patterns 150% for actual size.

Fluffy Fat Plushies

pages 66–69

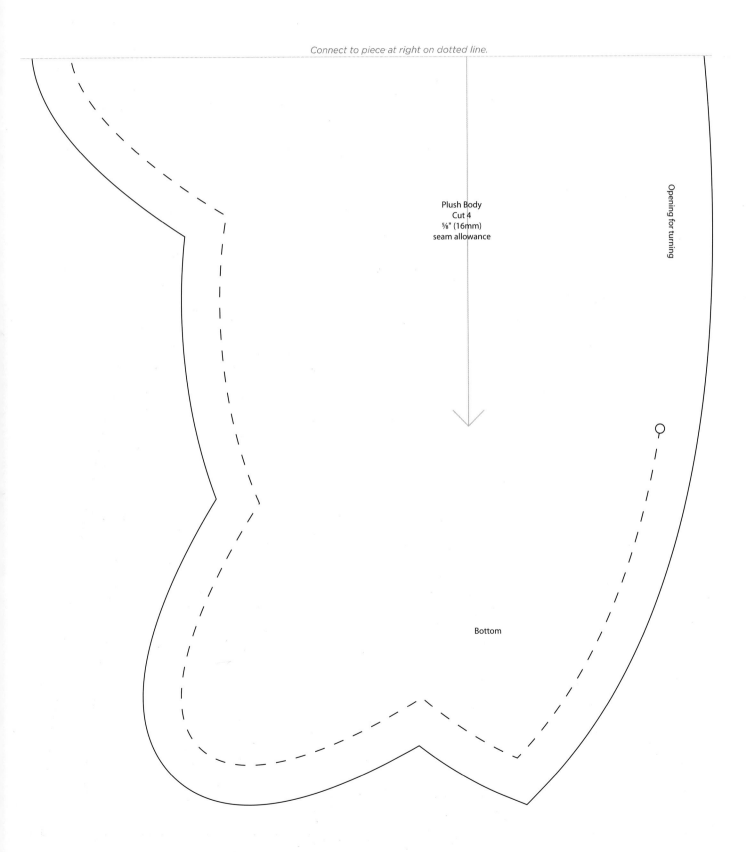

Connect to piece at right on dotted line.

Plush Body
Cut 4
⅝" (16mm)
seam allowance

Opening for turning

Bottom

Enlarge patterns 150% for actual size.

Fluffy Fat Plushies (continued)
pages 66–69

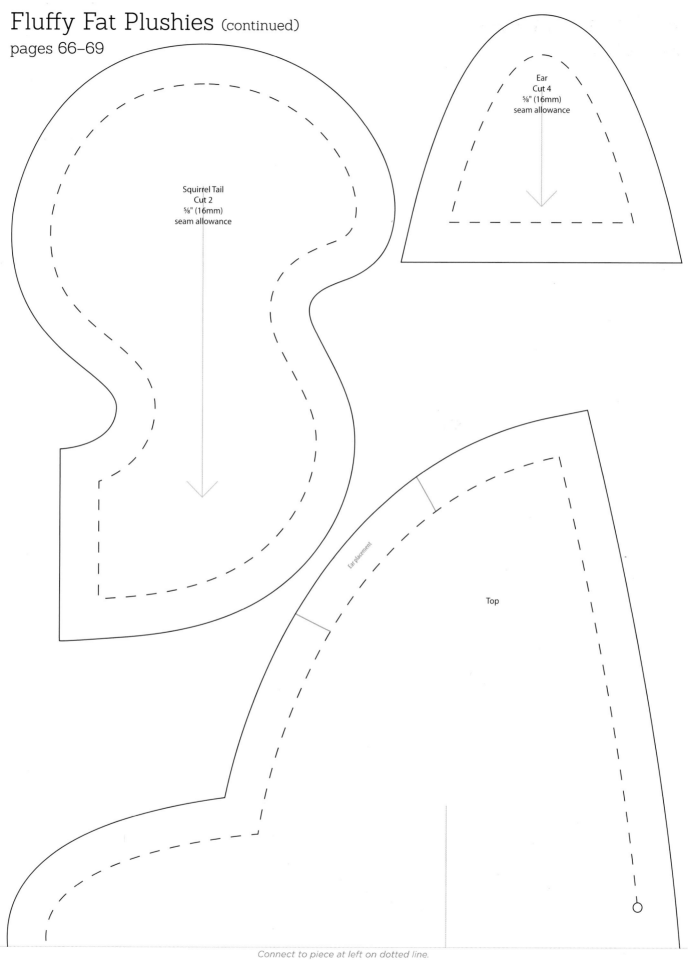

Squirrel Tail
Cut 2
⅝" (16mm)
seam allowance

Ear
Cut 4
⅝" (16mm)
seam allowance

Ear placement

Top

Connect to piece at left on dotted line.

Enlarge patterns 150% for actual size.

Fluffy Fat Plushies (continued)
pages 66–69

Squirrel & Cat face

Pig face

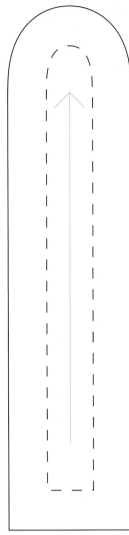

Pig Tail
Cut 2
⅝" (16mm)
seam allowance

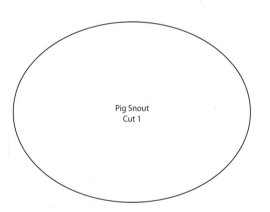

Pig Snout
Cut 1

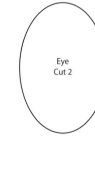

Eye
Cut 2

Pig Nostril
Cut 2

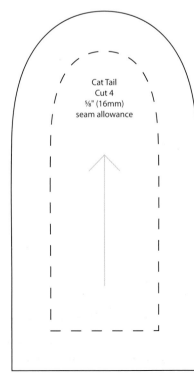

Cat Tail
Cut 4
⅝" (16mm)
seam allowance

Smile
Cut 1

Enlarge patterns 150% for actual size.

Plush Fruit Cubes
pages 70–72

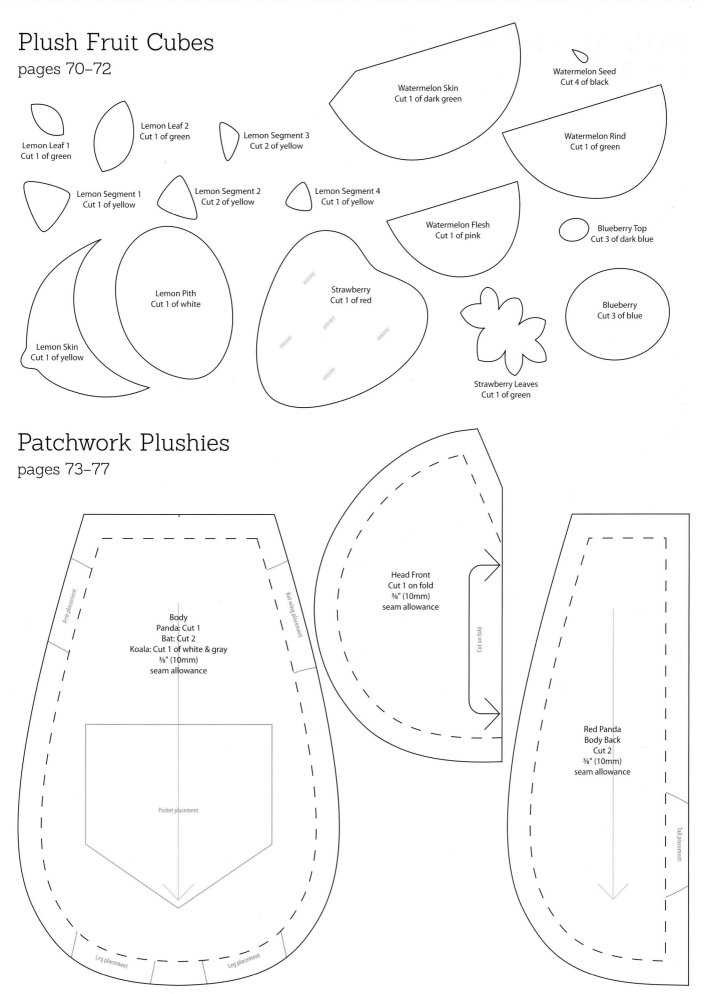

Watermelon Skin
Cut 1 of dark green

Watermelon Seed
Cut 4 of black

Lemon Leaf 2
Cut 1 of green

Lemon Segment 3
Cut 2 of yellow

Lemon Leaf 1
Cut 1 of green

Watermelon Rind
Cut 1 of green

Lemon Segment 1
Cut 1 of yellow

Lemon Segment 2
Cut 2 of yellow

Lemon Segment 4
Cut 1 of yellow

Watermelon Flesh
Cut 1 of pink

Blueberry Top
Cut 3 of dark blue

Lemon Pith
Cut 1 of white

Strawberry
Cut 1 of red

Blueberry
Cut 3 of blue

Lemon Skin
Cut 1 of yellow

Strawberry Leaves
Cut 1 of green

Patchwork Plushies
pages 73–77

Body
Panda: Cut 1
Bat: Cut 2
Koala: Cut 1 of white & gray
⅜" (10mm)
seam allowance

Arm placement

Bat wing placement

Pocket placement

Leg placement

Leg placement

Head Front
Cut 1 on fold
⅜" (10mm)
seam allowance

Cut on fold

Red Panda
Body Back
Cut 2
⅜" (10mm)
seam allowance

Tail placement

Enlarge patterns 150% for actual size.

Patchwork Plushies (continued)

pages 73–77

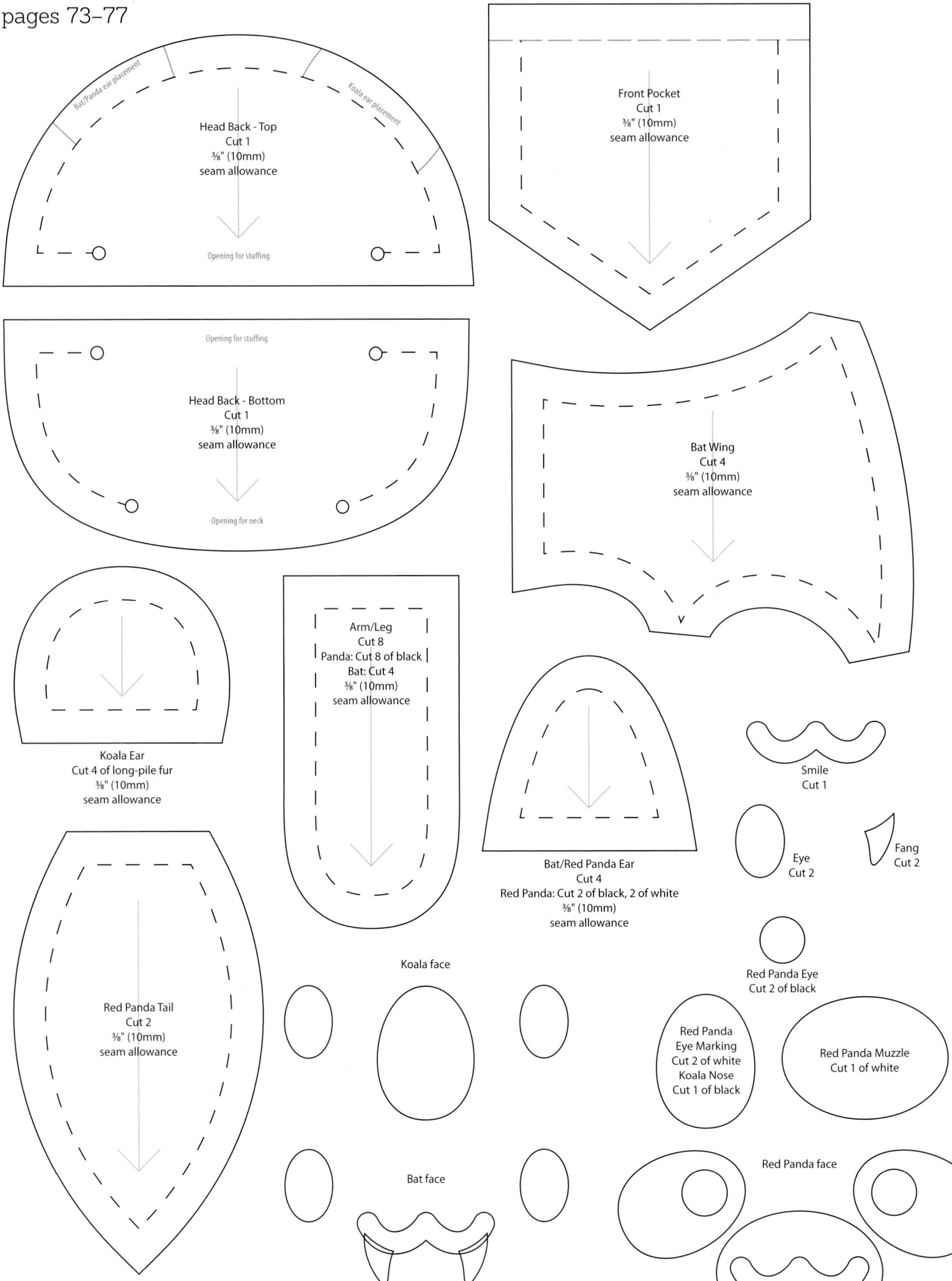

Bat/Panda ear placement

Koala ear placement

Head Back - Top
Cut 1
⅜" (10mm)
seam allowance

Opening for stuffing

Front Pocket
Cut 1
⅜" (10mm)
seam allowance

Opening for stuffing

Head Back - Bottom
Cut 1
⅜" (10mm)
seam allowance

Opening for neck

Bat Wing
Cut 4
⅜" (10mm)
seam allowance

Koala Ear
Cut 4 of long-pile fur
⅜" (10mm)
seam allowance

Arm/Leg
Cut 8
Panda: Cut 8 of black
Bat: Cut 4
⅜" (10mm)
seam allowance

Bat/Red Panda Ear
Cut 4
Red Panda: Cut 2 of black, 2 of white
⅜" (10mm)
seam allowance

Smile
Cut 1

Eye
Cut 2

Fang
Cut 2

Red Panda Eye
Cut 2 of black

Red Panda Tail
Cut 2
⅜" (10mm)
seam allowance

Koala face

**Red Panda
Eye Marking**
Cut 2 of white
Koala Nose
Cut 1 of black

Red Panda Muzzle
Cut 1 of white

Red Panda face

Bat face

Enlarge patterns 150% for actual size.

Lazy Body Pillow

pages 78–81

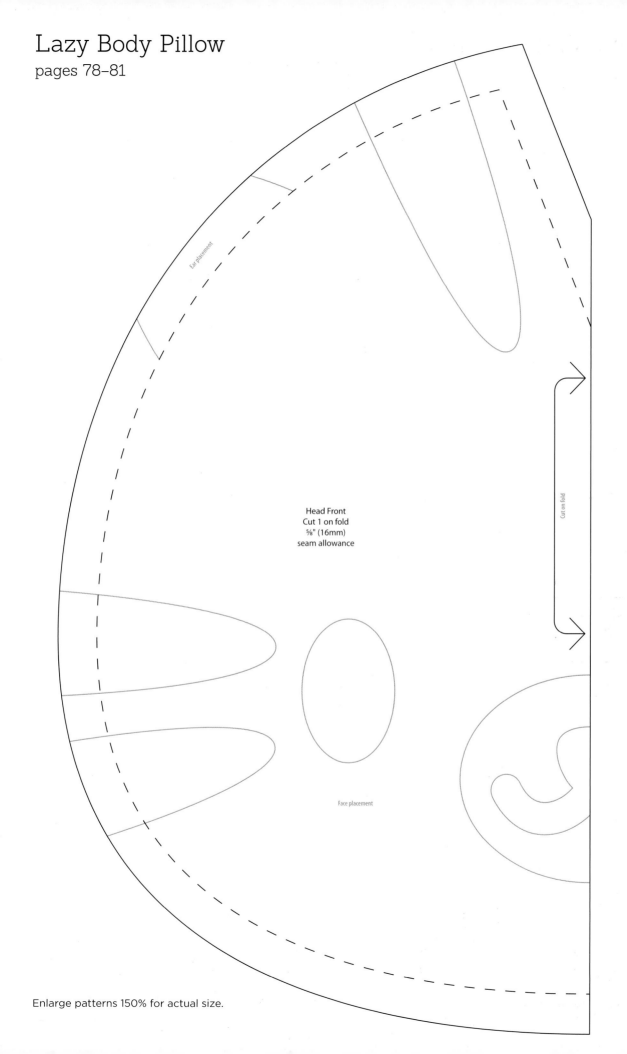

Ear placement

Head Front
Cut 1 on fold
⅝" (16mm)
seam allowance

Cut on fold

Face placement

Enlarge patterns 150% for actual size.

Lazy Body Pillow (continued)

pages 78–81

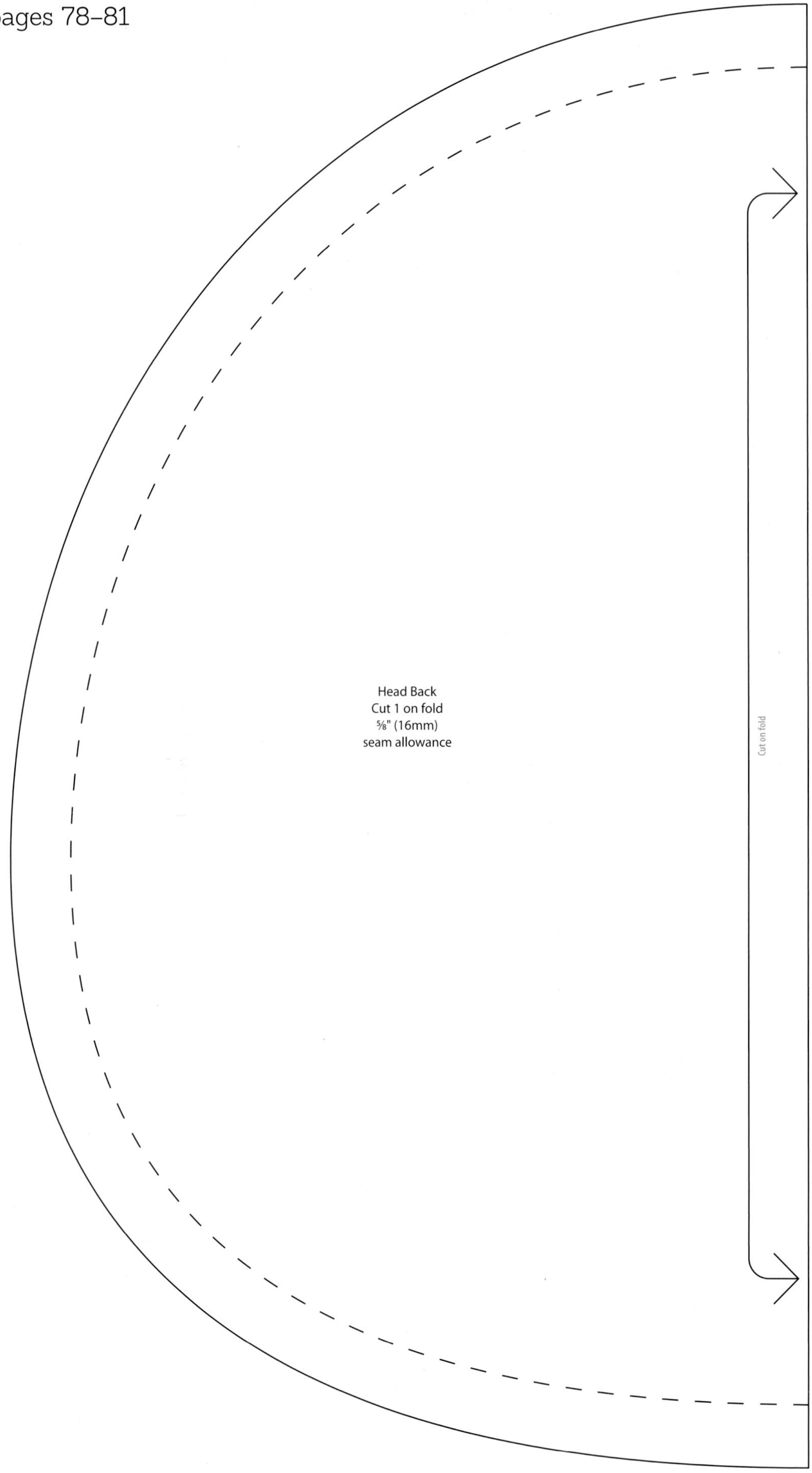

Head Back
Cut 1 on fold
⅝" (16mm)
seam allowance

Cut on fold

Enlarge patterns 150% for actual size.

Ocean Bed Burp Cloths

pages 84–85

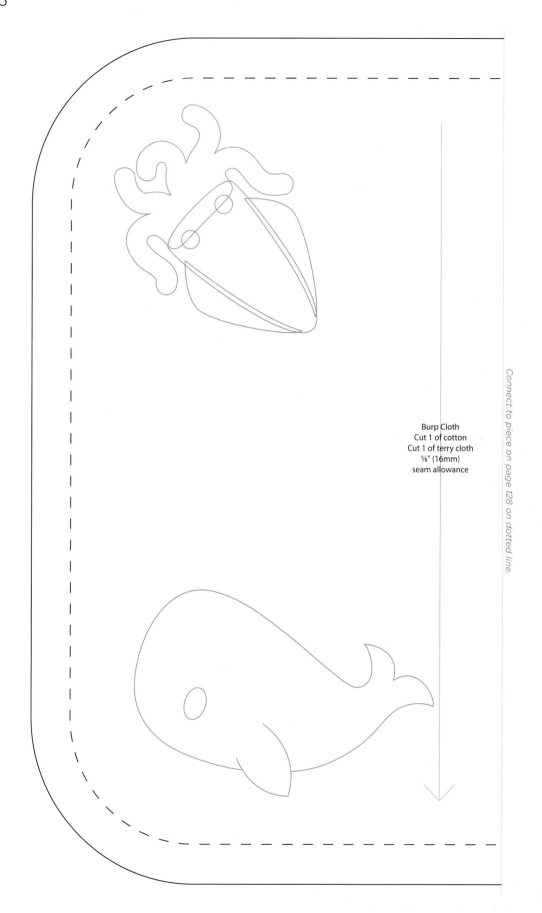

Burp Cloth
Cut 1 of cotton
Cut 1 of terry cloth
⅝" (16mm)
seam allowance

Connect to piece on page 128 on dotted line.

Enlarge patterns 150% for actual size.

Ocean Bed Burp Cloths (continued)
pages 84–85

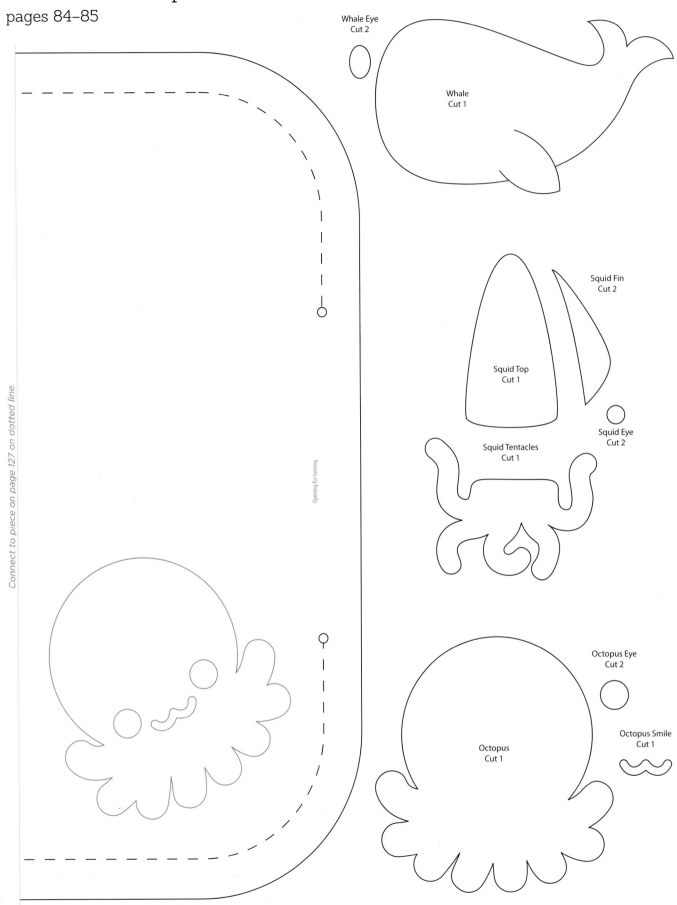

Whale Eye
Cut 2

Whale
Cut 1

Squid Fin
Cut 2

Squid Top
Cut 1

Squid Eye
Cut 2

Squid Tentacles
Cut 1

Octopus Eye
Cut 2

Octopus
Cut 1

Octopus Smile
Cut 1

Connect to piece on page 127 on dotted line.

Opening for turning

Enlarge patterns 150% for actual size.

Cuddly Creatures Hooded Towel

pages 86–88

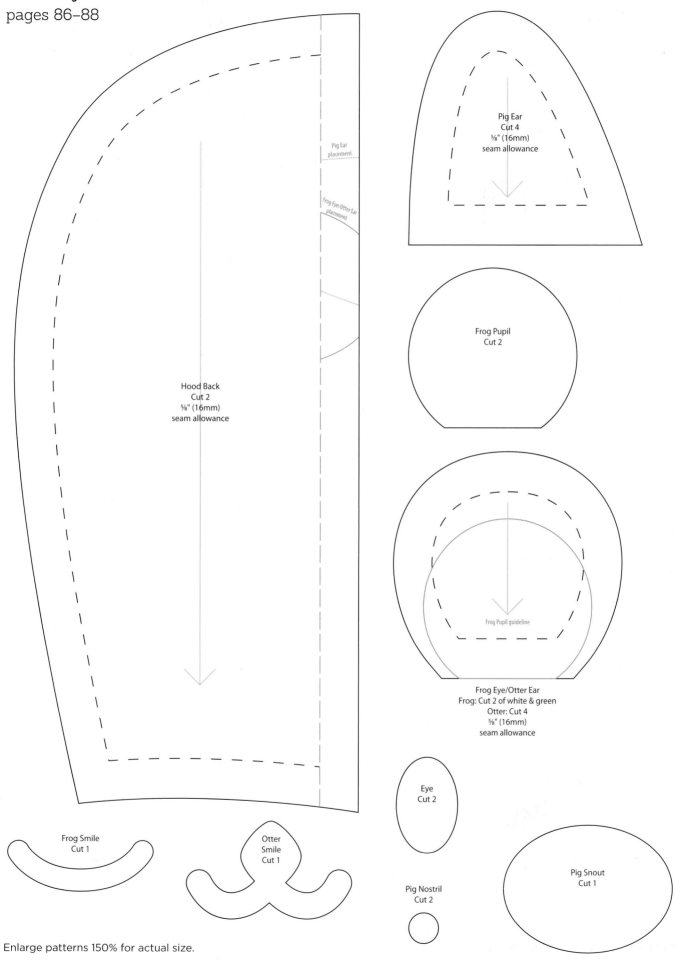

Pig Ear
Cut 4
⅝" (16mm)
seam allowance

Pig Ear
placement

Frog Eye/Otter Ear
placement

Hood Back
Cut 2
⅝" (16mm)
seam allowance

Frog Pupil
Cut 2

Frog Pupil guideline

Frog Eye/Otter Ear
Frog: Cut 2 of white & green
Otter: Cut 4
⅝" (16mm)
seam allowance

Frog Smile
Cut 1

Otter
Smile
Cut 1

Eye
Cut 2

Pig Nostril
Cut 2

Pig Snout
Cut 1

Enlarge patterns 150% for actual size.

Cuddly Creatures Hooded Towel (continued)
pages 86–88

Connect to piece at right on dotted line.

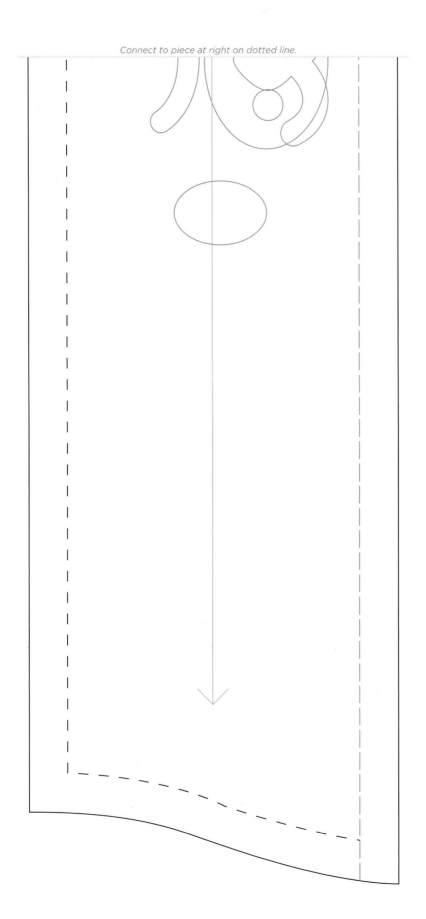

Enlarge patterns 150% for actual size.

Cuddly Creatures Hooded Towel (continued)

pages 86–88

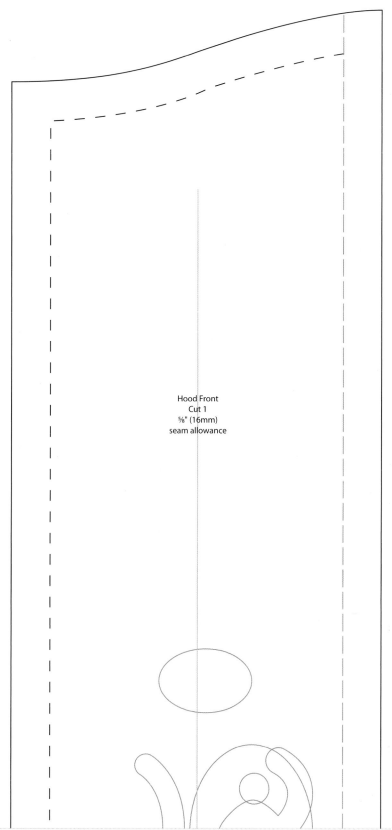

Hood Front
Cut 1
⅝" (16mm)
seam allowance

Connect to piece at left on dotted line.

Enlarge patterns 150% for actual size.

Cuddly Creatures Hooded Towel (continued)
pages 86–88

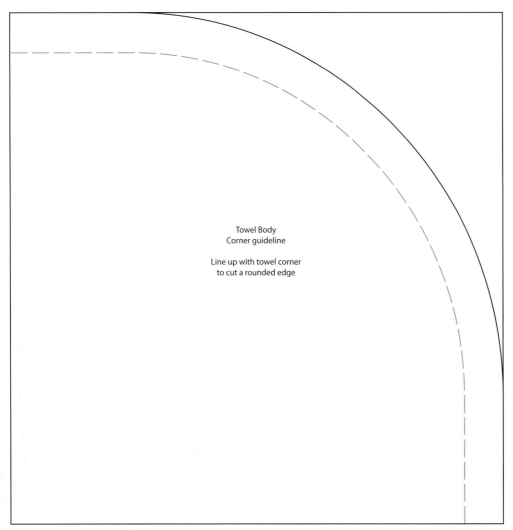

Towel Body
Corner guideline

Line up with towel corner
to cut a rounded edge

Cottony Clean Bibs
pages 89–91

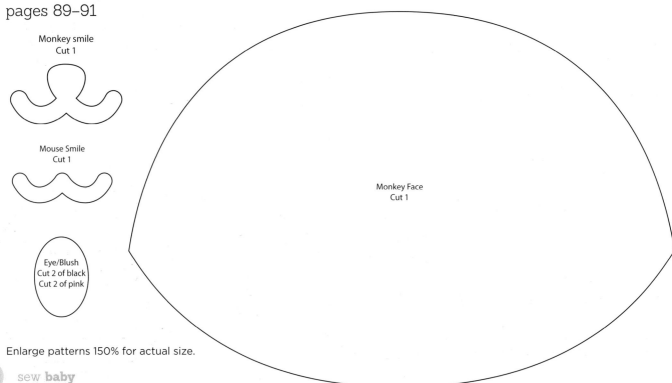

Monkey smile
Cut 1

Mouse Smile
Cut 1

Eye/Blush
Cut 2 of black
Cut 2 of pink

Monkey Face
Cut 1

Enlarge patterns 150% for actual size.

Cottony Clean Bibs (continued)
pages 89–91

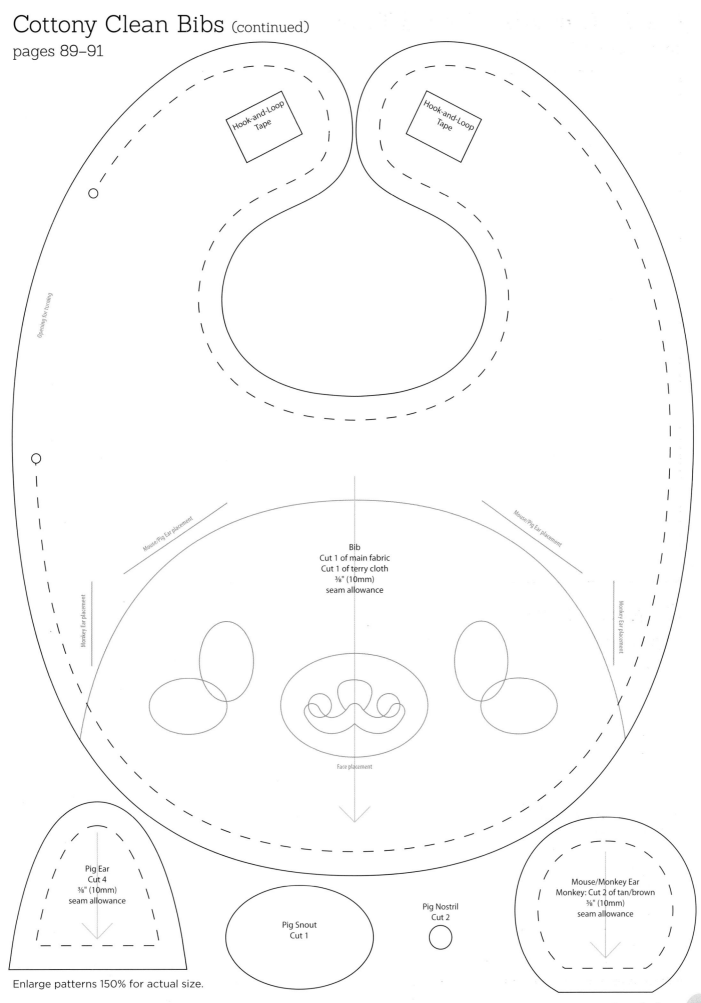

Hook-and-Loop Tape

Hook-and-Loop Tape

Opening for turning

Mouse/Pig Ear placement

Mouse/Pig Ear placement

Monkey Ear placement

Monkey Ear placement

Bib
Cut 1 of main fabric
Cut 1 of terry cloth
⅜" (10mm)
seam allowance

Face placement

Pig Ear
Cut 4
⅜" (10mm)
seam allowance

Pig Snout
Cut 1

Pig Nostril
Cut 2

Mouse/Monkey Ear
Monkey: Cut 2 of tan/brown
⅜" (10mm)
seam allowance

Enlarge patterns 150% for actual size.

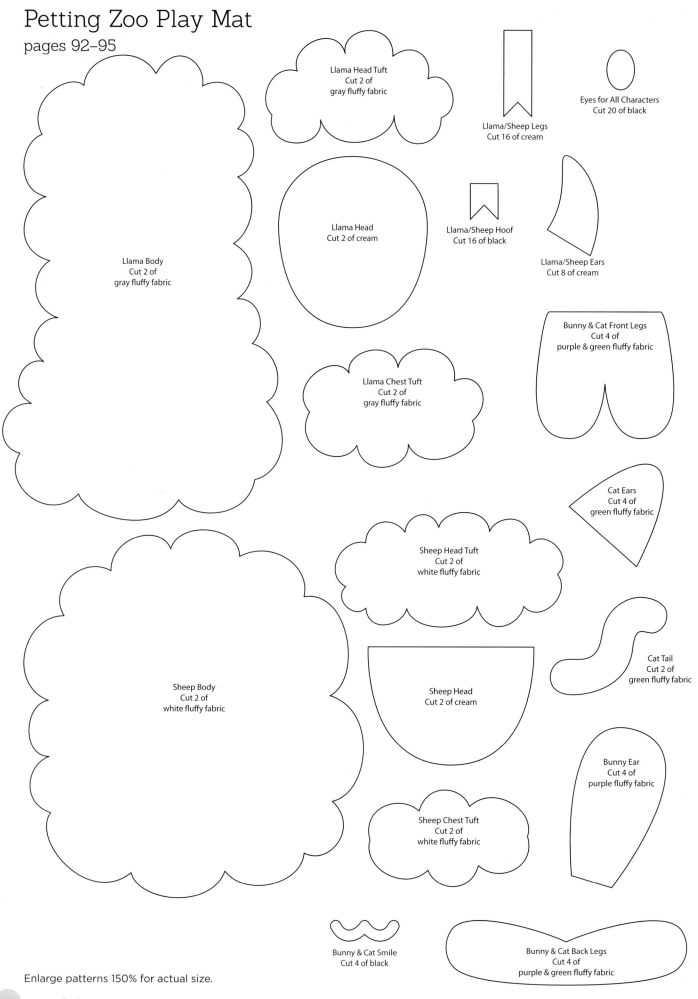

Petting Zoo Play Mat

pages 92–95

Llama Head Tuft
Cut 2 of
gray fluffy fabric

Llama/Sheep Legs
Cut 16 of cream

Eyes for All Characters
Cut 20 of black

Llama Head
Cut 2 of cream

Llama/Sheep Hoof
Cut 16 of black

Llama/Sheep Ears
Cut 8 of cream

Llama Body
Cut 2 of
gray fluffy fabric

Bunny & Cat Front Legs
Cut 4 of
purple & green fluffy fabric

Llama Chest Tuft
Cut 2 of
gray fluffy fabric

Cat Ears
Cut 4 of
green fluffy fabric

Sheep Head Tuft
Cut 2 of
white fluffy fabric

Cat Tail
Cut 2 of
green fluffy fabric

Sheep Body
Cut 2 of
white fluffy fabric

Sheep Head
Cut 2 of cream

Bunny Ear
Cut 4 of
purple fluffy fabric

Sheep Chest Tuft
Cut 2 of
white fluffy fabric

Bunny & Cat Smile
Cut 4 of black

Bunny & Cat Back Legs
Cut 4 of
purple & green fluffy fabric

Enlarge patterns 150% for actual size.

Petting Zoo Play Mat (continued)

pages 92–95

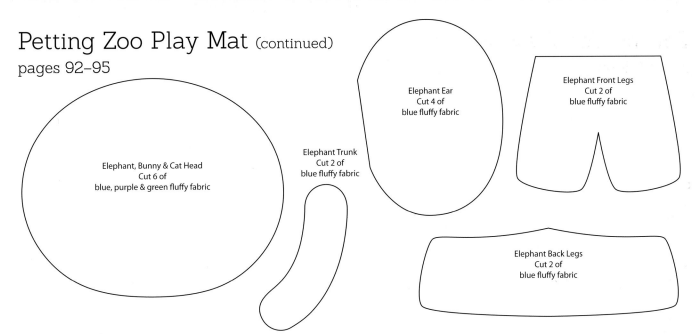

Elephant, Bunny & Cat Head
Cut 6 of
blue, purple & green fluffy fabric

Elephant Trunk
Cut 2 of
blue fluffy fabric

Elephant Ear
Cut 4 of
blue fluffy fabric

Elephant Front Legs
Cut 2 of
blue fluffy fabric

Elephant Back Legs
Cut 2 of
blue fluffy fabric

Sleek Diaper Bag

pages 96–100

Super Mom applique
Cut 1

Super Dad applique
Cut 1

Baby Jolly Roger applique
Cut 1

Enlarge patterns 150% for actual size.

Sleek Diaper Bag (continued)
pages 96–100

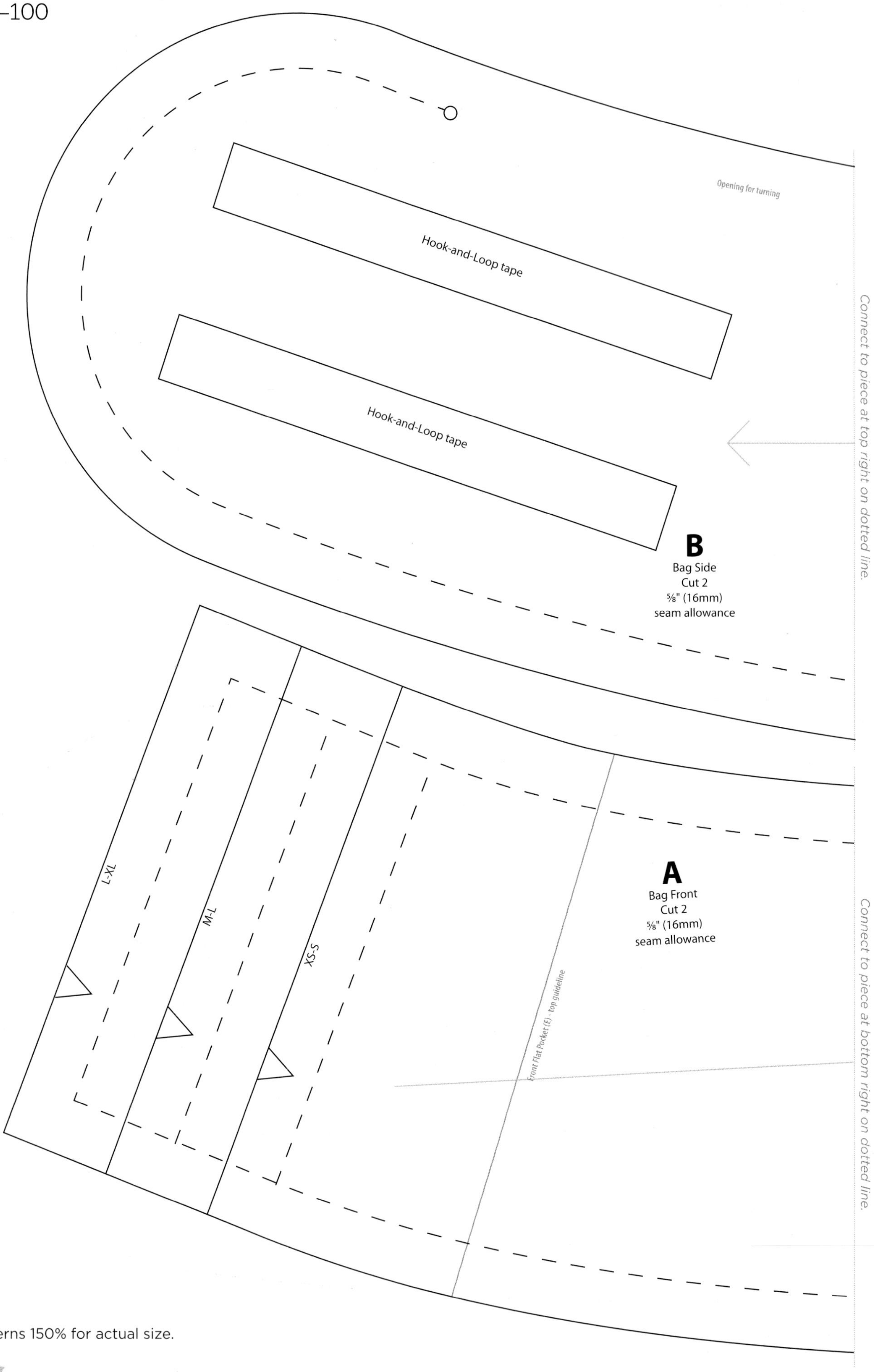

Hook-and-Loop tape

Hook-and-Loop tape

Opening for turning

B
Bag Side
Cut 2
⅝" (16mm)
seam allowance

Connect to piece at top right on dotted line.

L-XL

M-L

XS-S

Front Flat Pocket (F) - top guideline

A
Bag Front
Cut 2
⅝" (16mm)
seam allowance

Connect to piece at bottom right on dotted line.

Enlarge patterns 150% for actual size.

Sleek Diaper Bag (continued)
pages 96–100

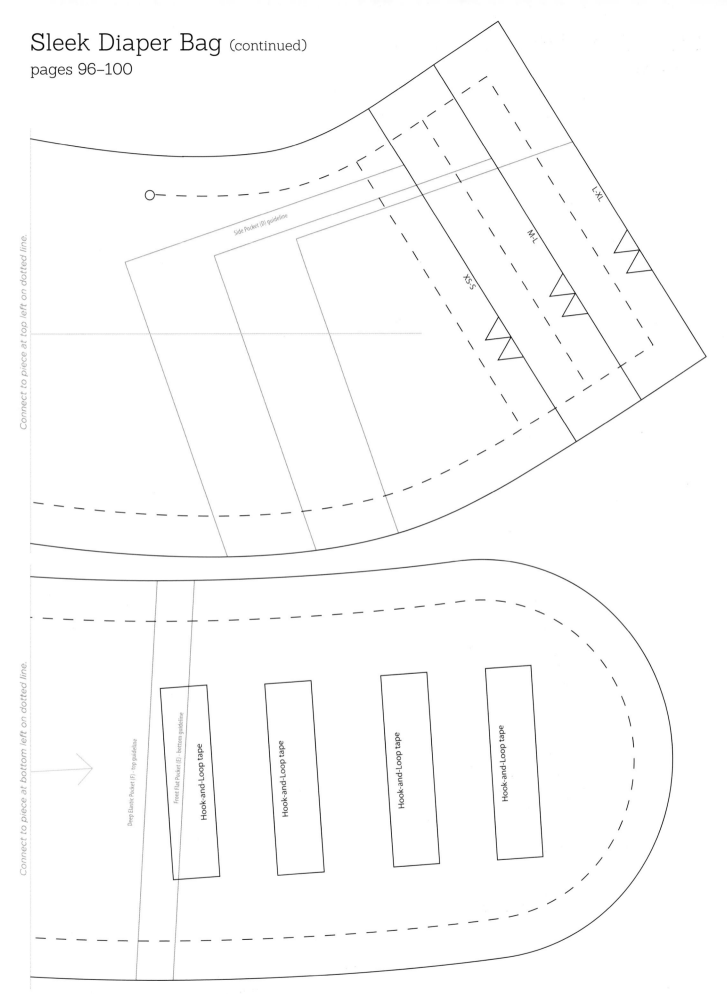

Side Pocket (D) guideline

L-XL

M-L

XS-S

Connect to piece at top left on dotted line.

Connect to piece at bottom left on dotted line.

Deep Elastic Pocket (F) - top guideline

Front Flat Pocket (E) - bottom guideline

Hook-and-Loop tape

Hook-and-Loop tape

Hook-and-Loop tape

Hook-and-Loop tape

Enlarge patterns 150% for actual size.

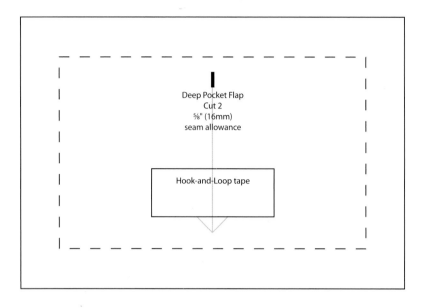

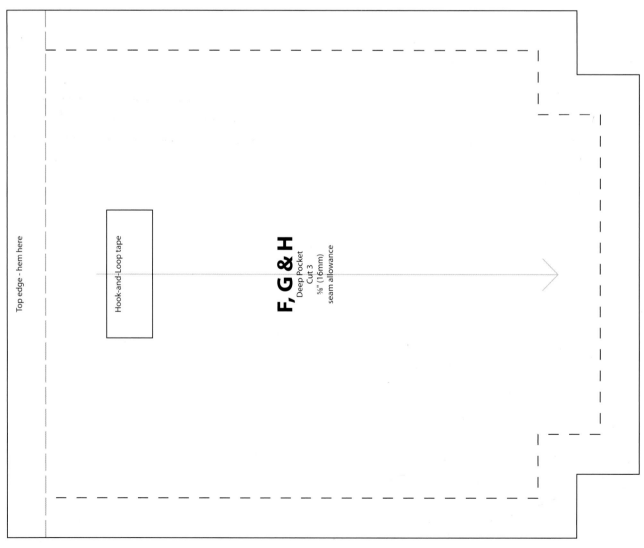

Enlarge patterns 150% for actual size.

Sleek Diaper Bag (continued)
pages 96–100

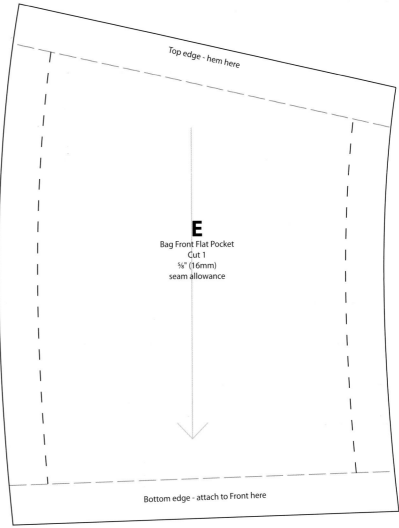

Top edge - hem here

E
Bag Front Flat Pocket
Cut 1
⅝" (16mm)
seam allowance

Bottom edge - attach to Front here

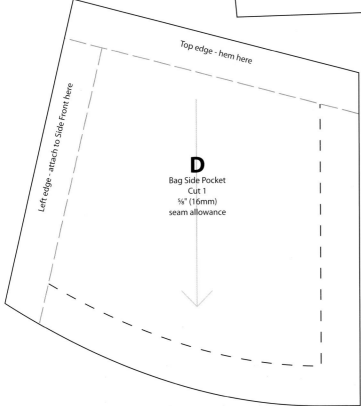

Top edge - hem here

Left edge - attach to Side Front here

D
Bag Side Pocket
Cut 1
⅝" (16mm)
seam allowance

Enlarge patterns 150% for actual size.

Sleek Diaper Bag (continued)
pages 96–100

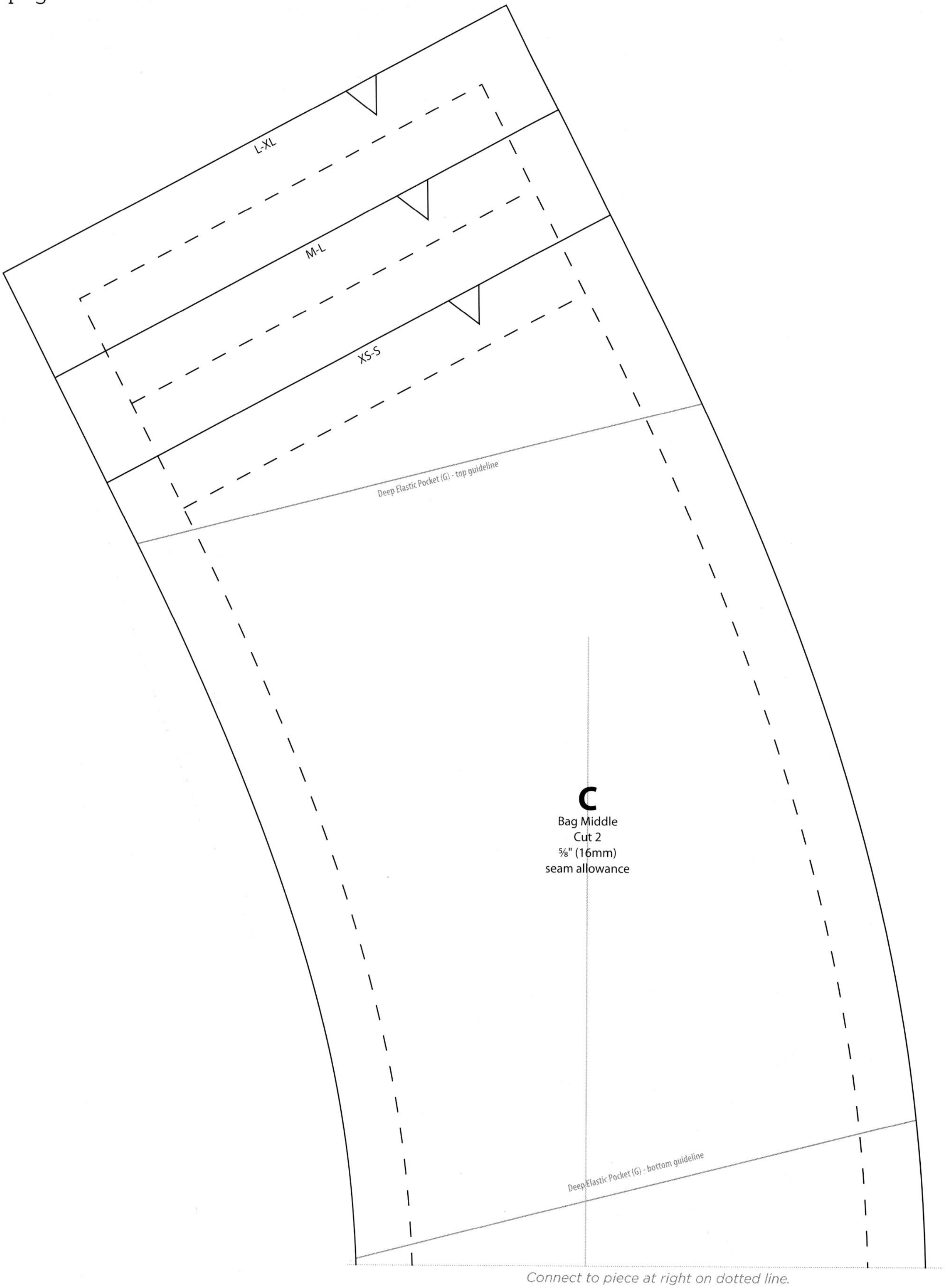

L-XL

M-L

XS-S

Deep Elastic Pocket (G) - top guideline

C
Bag Middle
Cut 2
⅝" (16mm)
seam allowance

Deep Elastic Pocket (G) - bottom guideline

Connect to piece at right on dotted line.

Enlarge patterns 150% for actual size.

Sleek Diaper Bag (continued)
pages 96–100

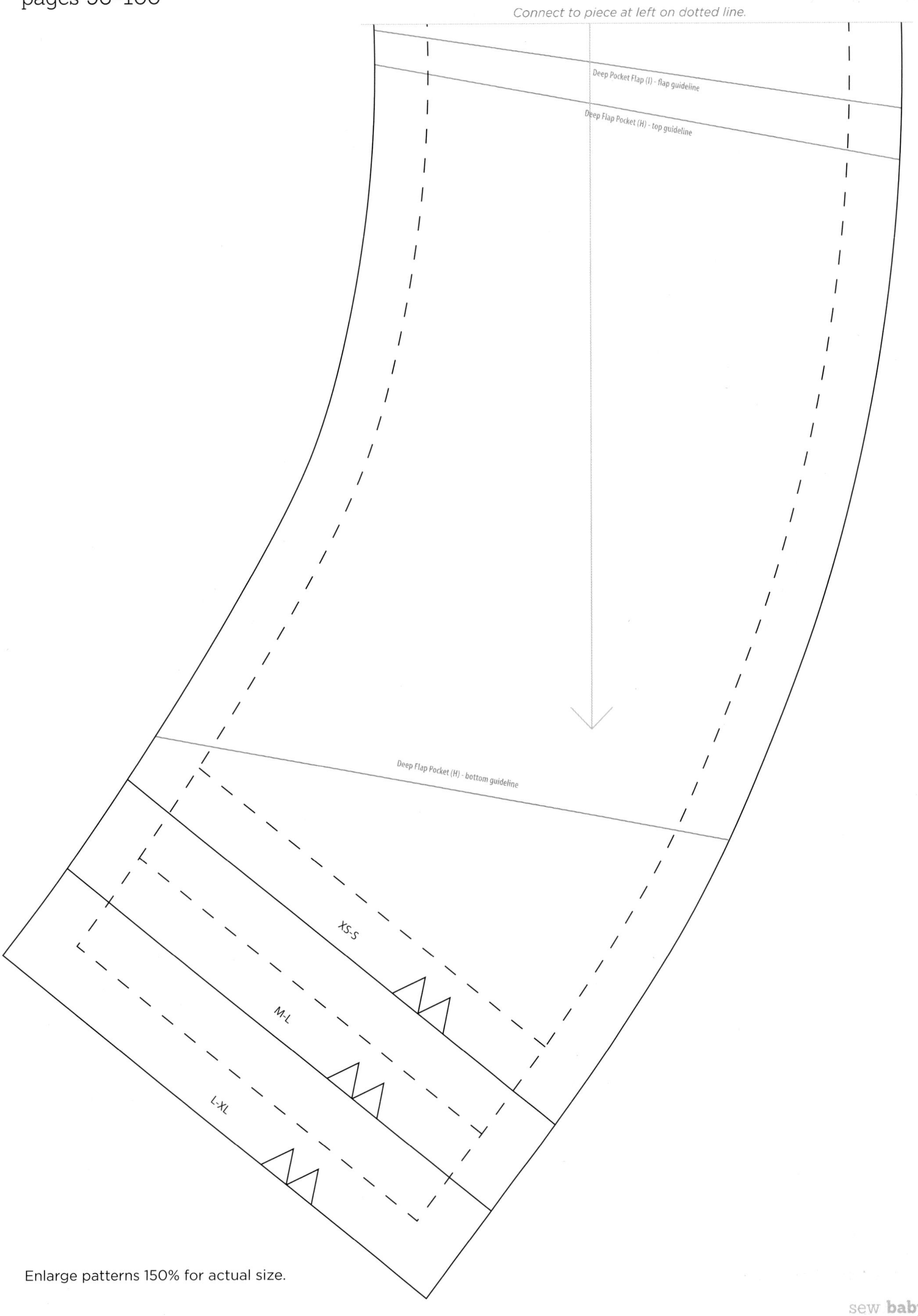

Connect to piece at left on dotted line.

Deep Pocket Flap (I) - flap guideline

Deep Flap Pocket (H) - top guideline

Deep Flap Pocket (H) - bottom guideline

XS-S

M-L

L-XL

Enlarge patterns 150% for actual size.

index

Note: Page numbers in *italics* indicate projects, and page numbers in **bold** indicate patterns.

ACQUISITION EDITOR
Kerri Landis

BOOK DESIGNER
Lindsay Hess

CONTRIBUTING PHOTOGRAPHERS
Lindsay Hess and Mallory Sensenig

COPY EDITORS
Paul Hambke and Heather Stauffer

COVER AND GALLERY PHOTOGRAPHER
Scott Kriner

DEVELOPMENTAL EDITOR
Kerri Landis

EDITOR
Katie Weeber

INDEXER
Jay Kreider

PROOFREADER
Lynda Jo Runkle

STEP-BY-STEP PHOTOGRAPHER
Matthew McClure

More Great Books from Design Originals

Sew Kawaii!
ISBN: 978-1-56523-568-7 **$19.95**

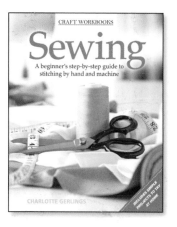

Sewing
ISBN: 978-1-56523-682-0 **$9.95**

Sew Your Own Pet Pillows
ISBN: 978-1-57421-343-0
DO3466 **$8.99**

Crochet Bouquet
ISBN: 978-1-57421-346-1
DO3469 **$12.99**

Just Like Me Crochet Patterns
ISBN: 978-1-57421-347-8
DO3470 **$12.99**

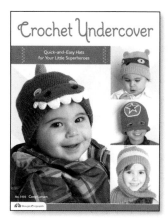

Crochet Undercover
ISBN: 978-1-57421-432-1
DO5403 **$12.99**

Steampunk Your Wardrobe
ISBN: 978-1-57421-417-8
DO5388 **$19.99**

Crazy Quilt Christmas Stockings
ISBN: 978-1-57421-360-7
DO3483 **$8.99**

Five-Minute Quilt Blocks
ISBN: 978-1-57421-420-8
DO5391 **$18.99**